My WHITE WIFE is a **RACIST?**

MW00881687

REALLY?

A Patriotic Look at Liberal Hypocrisy

ANTHONY L. THORNTON, PH.D.

Table of Contents

Dedication

This book is dedicated to all Americans. My wife and I want you to understand what we understand... the greatness of this country comes from individual initiative. Each of us contributes to the fabric of society and the unique American culture through hard work and perseverance. Our society as a whole benefits through the collective contributions of individual efforts. Our ideas, innovations, and productivity come from God-given individual talents and efforts. We are not all the same, nor will we ever be. Some of us contribute more to this society than others. Those who do should also be allowed to enjoy the fruits of their labor. Those who choose not to contribute, through their own inaction, should experience the consequences of their choices. Those who cannot contribute through no fault of their own, we will be there for you because we are the most generous nation on the face of this earth.

We live in a time where the state (our government) wants to treat us like sheep. They punish the successful and reward the lazy to keep us under the shepherd's watch. Don't let them. Individual responsibility is the expected norm in our society. Individuals who exhibit bad behavior with reckless decisions should suffer the consequences. Free market capitalism enables America to compete globally. If you are looking for a handout... sorry. In our America, inspiration, innovation, and initiative shall be rewarded. It's time for us to get back to the basic fundamental reason of why America excels. America works because Americans work. We work hard, and we enjoy it because we know we will be rewarded. This is what the American Dream means.

Liberal interpretation of the above dedication -- The author must be a racist.

Foreword

This is a story about a white woman who meets a black man, falls in love, and marries him. They live happily ever after.

Life is pretty simple when you put it in simple terms. No need for complex analysis. Like most Americans, I believe common sense can take you a long way if you just apply it to your daily life. We have all heard of the K.I.S.S. principle... Keep It Simple, Stupid. The problem with today's world is that K.I.S.S. no longer applies, especially in regards to religion, politics, economics, and race relations.

This is a story of a journey of two people. Two people from differing backgrounds, who come together and discover a world turned upside down, a world in which right is wrong and wrong is rewarded. Their journey will show you the hypocrisy of economics, the hypocrisy of politics, and the hypocrisy of race relations. Despite all of it, we realize one truth... what we do here and now only matters to those generations who will follow us. Can we "fundamentally transform" America back to a free society? We say yes, and we can point with comedic ridicule to those not willing to return to the basic foundations that created this great country. This book was written for conservative entertainment in a time of serious deliberation on the future direction of this country. As you read this book, you will often come across the term *poppycock*. I decided to use this term instead of the more literal translation "**B**ovine **S**not" or B.S. for short.

Recently, I came across an article entitled "A Black Man, the Progressive's Perfect Trojan Horse," written by Lloyd Marcus, another TEA Party patriot who just happens to be black. In the article, Mr. Marcus states the following:

> *"The mainstream liberal media continues to portray all who oppose Obama in any way as racist. Despite a list of failed policies, overreaches into the private sector, violations of the Constitution and planned destructive legislation too numerous to mention, many Americans are still fearful of criticizing our first black president. Incredible."*

I couldn't be any clearer myself. The time for fear is over. The policies of the current Administration's liberal agenda are crazy, irrational, and dare I say it, ridiculous. Actually, it would be comical, if the consequences of continuing them weren't so dangerous to our future as a freedom-loving nation. You be the judge.

- Anthony L. Thornton, Ph.D.

Final note: Half of our net proceeds from this book we intend to donate to the Wounded Warrior Project.

Wounded Warrior Project™ (WWP) began when several veterans and friends, moved by stories of the first wounded service members returning home from Afghanistan and Iraq, took action to help others in need. What started as a program to provide comfort items to wounded service members has grown into a complete rehabilitative effort to assist warriors as they recover and transition back to civilian life.

http://www.woundedwarriorproject.org/

Acknowledgements

I would like to thank Gretchen Mott, my mother-in-law, for her tireless editorial support in reviewing this book. In addition, I am indebted to Gene and Melanie Peak for their candid review and editorial comments. I would like to acknowledge Jodi Newton for her fine photography used on the cover of this book. She can be reached at:

www.jodinewton.com

Finally, I have been encouraged by a number of friends and neighbors to finish this book. This has been a labor of love and without their support, I could not have completed this project.

Chapter I

MEET GRASSHOPPER

The Rules

1. Don't believe everything you see, because your eyes will lie to you.

2. Don't believe everything you hear, because your ears will lie to you.

3. Believe in your nose. If it doesn't smell right, it ain't right. Trust your nose.

Here she is... by the way she doesn't smoke. That fake cigarette was Photoshopped in after the picture was taken. Rule number 1: Don't believe everything you see because sometimes your eyes will lie to you. Rule number 2: Don't believe everything you hear because sometimes your ears will lie to you. Rule number 3: Don't believe everything you smell because... never mind, your nose doesn't lie. Rule number 3 Revised: Believe in your nose. If it doesn't smell right, it ain't right... trust your nose. We will revisit these rules throughout this book. You will discover that your nose is a good guide and common-sense compass.

The Meeting

It was March 17, 2004 when Lex, a colleague of mine at the aerospace firm where we worked, contacted me and suggested we meet for a drink after work. Lex is a professional, well-dressed, perfectly manicured, six-foot tall black male, who on occasion likes to flaunt his disposable income by going out to an upper-end bar, sip on a couple of glasses of wine after work and maybe enjoy a nice dinner. Lex is what one would call a metrosexual... a guy who pays attention to detail, has a flare about style and fashion, likes nice things, and is meticulous about neatness. Once he showed me his walk-in closet. Amazing! It looked like a Hollywood movie set where a rich tycoon employs a butler who has every item of clothing placed for him. Suit coats perfectly arranged by color, pants hung in a line like a department store, and shoes placed on their respective shelf. However, despite these idiosyncrasies, Lex was not effeminate, nor gay. He was just a well-tailored brother from the South who earned his way to success and enjoyed the finer things in life.

Lex and I hit it off a few years earlier when we both were selected to serve on a team to consolidate the merger of three aerospace companies during the summer of 2000. That was an experience in how NOT to bring three different company cultures together. For those of you who are *Star Trek: Next Generation* television fans, you will recall the most feared enemy for the crew members of the U.S.S. Enterprise was the Borg... a colony of cybernetic organisms, half-human, half machine all controlled by a central mind/computer. The Borg use abduction and assimilation to conquer an enemy. Their goal is to include your biological and technological distinctiveness into the collective hive mind in their pursuit of "perfection." Once you are assimilated, all members of the collective hive know everything you know instantaneously. In so doing, they can easily defeat any adversary. *"Resistance is futile... you will be assimilated."* was the clarion warning given when the Borg attacked. That was the attitude and the philosophy of the lead management company in Fort Worth, Texas where Lex worked and they were ruthless in consolidating the three aerospace companies. I originally worked in California in the Advanced Development group in Palmdale, California, and we, along with the aerospace company in Marietta, Georgia were being assimilated. Obviously I surrendered and became a good Borg, because I ended up in Fort Worth less than a year later.

During the assimilation process, Lex and I, being the only two blacks on the consolidation team, naturally migrated toward each other and became good friends. We were in our mid-forties, single, self-sufficient, and worked in a very tough cyclic industry notorious for laying people off during the lean times. If you could survive the downturns in the aerospace industry, you were good. Lex was a mathematician who liked formulas and process. He worked in the business development side of the house, and his attention to detail served him well.

I, on the other hand, was on the engineering side of the house. I received my undergraduate degree from the University of Colorado in Aerospace Engineering Sciences in the winter of 1978. I went on to obtain my Master's degree in Engineering from Stanford. After spending several years working for a national security high technology firm in New Mexico, I decided to pursue my Doctorate, which I obtained from Purdue University from the School of Aeronautics and Astronautics. My area of specialty was computational fluid dynamics. Speaking of fluid dynamics, unlike my wine sipping friend Lex, my preferred drink was Jack and Coke.

Lex and I would occasionally meet after work just to hang out and catch-up on things. He always knew where to go and if there was a new place with a nice bar or restaurant, Lex would check it out. There were usually three requirements for Lex to refer a place... nice ambience, well-stocked bar, and the availability of mature, professional, attractive women.

On this particular day, he asked me if I had ever been to a place called Michael's Restaurant. I stated I had never been to or heard of the place. He said it was nice and had a cool vibe. I agreed to meet him in the parking lot after work so I could follow him to Michael's, which was near the aerospace plant off West 7th street in Fort Worth.

As we entered into the restaurant, both he and I immediately noticed two women to our right talking. The woman facing us as we entered was a stunning raven-haired siren with legs to die for. I looked at Lex and said, "I like this place already." Lex and I promptly stepped up to the bar next to the women and ordered a couple of drinks for us. Lex and I had an understanding whenever we went out... we would let things happen naturally. We never went to a bar with the intention to meet and pick up women... we always went with the intent to soak in the atmosphere and enjoy our "guy time" together. If we happened to meet some new people while we were there, male or female, fine. We never went for the hunt as most guys do. Neither one of us ever had any problems finding a date and neither one of us was interested in a serious relationship. We were too focused on our professional lives to chase women.

So, Lex and I sat there for a while catching up on company news completely ignoring the women talking next to us. We both commented on the attractiveness of the raven-haired woman who seemed oblivious to our presence. As I was about to order another drink, the woman in the group whose back had been to us the entire time, turned around to face me and placed her hand on my knee and said "I just wanted to tell you that you are the cutest young thing." My first thought was, okay – today is St. Patty's day, how much has this woman had to drink already? Instead, I answered, "Thanks, but I'm older than I look." She smiled, probably the best smile I had ever seen in my lifetime, laughed and said "Oh honey, I'm not trying to pick you up. I'm married and I am old enough to be your mother." I laughed and said, "I don't think so. How old are you?" She said in her slow Texas drawl, "Honey I'm 48 years old!" I smiled and said "I'm 47." Her face showed disbelief, "There is NO way you are 47 years old!" I laughed again and asked her if she was from Texas? "Hell yes!" she exclaimed with pride "and where are you from?" I said I was born in California. She smiled and flatly stated, "Oh, you are from the Socialist Republic of California." I stopped and said "What?" She continued, "You know, that's really a great state. It's too bad the liberals who live there have ruined it!"

I've known this woman for all of 2 seconds, and we are talking politics. I thought to myself, this is going to be fun.

I had found a political foe and what the heck; she was a friend to the raven-haired beauty who still hadn't noticed us. Game on!

The Other Side of the Story

I went to Michael's with my friend, the raven-haired beauty (RHB from now on) to sit with her until a friend of hers from Waco, Texas arrived to join us. I rarely went out for a drink after work with friends. I was married and was still home-schooling my special-needs adopted child. However, on this particular occasion, RHB really wanted some company and begged me to tag along until her friend arrived. While we were waiting, these two professional white-collar types, nice looking young men came into the establishment. I didn't give them much notice initially.

After some time chitchatting, the girl from Waco arrived along with her boyfriend. Problem was I immediately recognized her boyfriend and I knew he was married. Yikes! In my feeble attempt to not be seen by the married boyfriend, I turned to one of the young men who were sitting right beside me, and I just had to tell him that he was the nicest looking YOUNG man. He said something to the effect that he wasn't as young as I thought. Well, I let him know that first of all I wasn't trying to pick him up and second of all, I was old enough to be his mother. Yes, maybe a young mother, but a mother nonetheless and then I gave him that motherly pat on his knee. I just thought he was darling, in that motherly sort of way. Some people claim I was being a "Cougar" hitting on what I perceived to be a younger man. It was 2004 and I'm not sure the term Cougar even existed at the time. Besides, do you know anyone who uses the "I'm old enough to be your mother!" line to pick someone up?

Once we established that I was wrong on the age thing, he just looked at me and said something to the effect of "You are so Texan!" and I said "And you are so... what exactly?" He said he was originally from California, and I followed that up with "Oh, so you're from the Socialist Republic of California?" I got a strange look from him and his friend. This led to a conversation on politics. I was a Bush girl, and proud of it. I must tell you that these two gentlemen were Black (Is that the proper term nowadays? I can't keep up). So, in my Texas style, I asked "Why do Blacks always vote in unison? Ya'll are like sheep. No other race does that." I continued, "You could spot me from across the room and you would have no idea how I vote. But I could be 95% sure that I would be right about the both of you!" Once again I got the strange look. Game on. It was going to be an interesting ride. And I wasn't afraid to ask questions.

The Challenge

While I don't recall all of the details, this woman whose name I learned was Glenna started railing into me about liberalism, and how it stifles and kills businesses. She said she was a George Bush fan and I asked "Why, because he is from Texas?" she said "No, because he is Republican." I gave Lex this perplexed look that said "Is this lady for real?" It was clear from her attitude, confident demeanor, and pride that she meant what she said. I stepped back for a second and asked "Why do you like Bush?" She replied, "Because he has kept us safe since 9-11." I stated

"That might be true, but he has also stepped on our rights as citizens to keep us safe by approving the Patriot Act. I think it was Benjamin Franklin who stated, *"He that gives up his liberty for security, deserves neither."* In addition, Bush is spending money and increasing our debt as a nation because of the war in Iraq, which, frankly, we didn't have to enter into because we already had Saddam Hussein contained. By the way, where are those weapons of mass destruction Saddam had stashed away?"

What Glenna didn't know at the time was that while I didn't particularly like many of Bush's policies, I didn't really hate George W. Bush. I felt he was a nice guy who had excelled well beyond his capacity, and despite what I thought were his many flaws, I had no doubt that George W. Bush loved this country and he respected the men and women who served in the armed forces. That was important to me since my father spent his career in the military. I believe a turning point for me was the fantastic speech that President Bush gave to the nation after 9-11. No matter what you felt about him personally, he did what a great leader is supposed to do in trying times... he brought the people together and rallied our will to stand up to this new threat to our nation.

As a black male, I grew up as a Democrat. My father was a 27-year career enlisted man in the Air Force and he had experienced some tough times in the service when there were still issues with segregation. My father was one of the first black men to reach Chief Master Sergeant in the Air Force, which taught me a lesson on the value of perseverance. He was a hard worker and a good provider for his family. My two sisters and I never wanted for anything, and my mother was the epitome of the stay-at-home "Leave it to Beaver" mom (sans pearl necklace) during our early childhood that liberal women nowadays demonize.

So, I was raised a Democrat because the whole family was Democrat. We never really talked about politics in our family. It wasn't something even casually discussed that I can recall. I think the main reason being a Democrat felt right to me was because I grew up in the turbulent 60's. At that time, many of our "leaders" including John F. Kennedy, Martin Luther King, Jr., and Bobby Kennedy were assassinated. It seemed to me at the time that the Democrats were trying to change the world for the better and some unknown force was taking them out, one by one. Of course, back then at the age of 12, I was naive to the policies of both parties; nor did I understand the real differences between the political parties. Black folks were focused on the civil rights movement. I recall the Mexico City Olympics when Tommie Smith and John Carlos raised their black-gloved hands on the podium during the playing of our National Anthem after receiving their gold and silver medals in the 200-meter dash. It was shocking to me at the time that these young men had the courage to tell the world that there was a problem with race relations in the good 'ole U.S. of A. Bob Beamon could shatter the world's record in the long jump, but couldn't jump out of his black skin to avoid being treated like a second-class citizen in his country of origin. Those were indeed turbulent times.

Despite all of that, it was also a time of tremendous optimism. On July 24, 1969 this nation fulfilled a vision to place a man on the moon and return him safely back to earth. Three days prior, on July 21, Neil Armstrong changed my life. I decided I wanted to be an aerospace engineer. I thought that maybe I could be the first black astronaut. At 13, I aspired to be more than what I was. Having grown up on Air Force bases most of my life, I was always near aircraft and fascinated by flight. When we lived in Shreveport, Louisiana, I was amazed at the size of the B-52 Bombers at Barksdale Air Force Base as they lumbered down the runway only to gracefully take to the sky. To me, they seemed to defy physics - how could anything that large get off the ground? I was determined to learn how it was possible.

It was a good thing that I had an affinity for math and science: otherwise having aspirations for engineering would have been short-lived. Like most young kids, I used to change my career aspirations from astronaut, to astronomer, and frequently to aquanaut thanks to Jacques-Yves Cousteau. For me, it was always about exploring the unknown. There has always been this need in me to know more, to learn more, and to experience more - traits I hope will stay with me until I die.

Wanting to learn more, I pressed Glenna and asked her why she was a Republican. She droned on and on about limited government and reduced spending while I countered with the fact that President Bush was expanding government and spending like a drunken sailor (with all due respect to drunken sailors). The details are a blur to me now, but Glenna didn't like the fact that I could easily rail on President Bush and his policies. Of course, she brought up President Bill Clinton and his lack of character and personal integrity. I, like most Democrats, excused

Clinton's bad behavior because he was our first black president... okay, not really, but we all thought that Clinton was a cool dude.

Glenna and I bantered back and forth over Democrats versus Republicans for quite a while. It became obvious that this was not going to get resolved in one night. We were going to have to continue our arguments/debates for a later time because clearly, in my opinion, this woman needed an education. Interestingly enough, our debate had gotten so intense, I completely forgot about RHB. It was a good thing, too, since Lex and I found out much later that RHB was nothing more than a money-grubbing, psychopath who could easily be bought by anyone making over $300K a year. RHB was currently "in love" with a rich married man who kept her on the side. Wow, what a waste!

Ms. Glenna and I exchanged business cards and agreed to continue the debate via email.

The Arguments

Republicans vs. Democrats

1. **It's not easy being Green.**

2. **Save first, purchase later.**

3. **You must put in the effort to achieve your goals in life.**

The following day, I received an e-mail from Glenna which really ticked me off. This, probably more than anything else, caused me to realize that people see the world only from their perspective. It doesn't matter that a different perspective may open your eyes to a different reality. Everyone thinks his or her own perspective is ground truth. I was guilty of believing that my reality was truth. Remember Rule # 1.

So Glenna sent me an Internet story. This particular story has seen several different versions circulating around the Internet. You may have seen a variation or two that continually get updated. Here is the first message this crazy white woman from Texas sent me in 2004:

OLD VERSION:

The Ant works hard in the withering heat all summer long, building his house and laying up supplies for the winter. The Grasshopper thinks he's a fool and laughs and dances and plays the summer away. Come winter, the Ant is warm and well fed. The Grasshopper has no food or shelter, so he dies out in the cold.

MORAL OF THE STORY: *Be responsible for yourself!*

MODERN VERSION:

The Ant works hard in the withering heat all summer long, building his house and laying up supplies for the winter. The Grasshopper thinks he's a fool and laughs and dances and plays the summer away. Come winter, the shivering Grasshopper calls a press conference and demands to know why the Ant should be allowed to be warm and well fed while others are cold and starving.

CBS, NBC, and ABC show up to provide pictures of the shivering Grasshopper next to a video of the Ant in his comfortable home with a table filled with food. America is stunned by the sharp contrast. How can this be that in a country of such wealth, this poor Grasshopper is allowed to suffer so?

Kermit the Frog appears on Oprah with the Grasshopper, and everybody cries when they sing, "It's Not Easy Being Green."

Jesse Jackson stages a demonstration in front of the Ant's house where the news stations film the group singing, "We shall overcome." Jesse then has the group kneel down to pray to God for the Grasshopper's sake.

Tom Daschle & John Kerry exclaim in an interview with Peter Jennings that the Ant has gotten rich off the back of the Grasshopper, and both call for an immediate tax hike on the Ant to make him pay his "fair share."

Finally, the EEOC drafts the "Economic Equity and Anti-Ant Act," retroactive to the beginning of the summer. The Ant is fined for failing to hire a proportionate number of green bugs and, having nothing left to pay his retroactive taxes, his home is confiscated by the government. Hillary gets her old law firm to represent the Grasshopper in defamation suit against the Ant, and the case is tried before a panel of federal judges that Bill appointed from a list of single-parent welfare recipients. The Ant loses the case.

The story ends as we see the Grasshopper finishing up the last bits of the Ant's food while the government house he is in, which just happens to be the Ant's old house, crumbles around him because he doesn't maintain it. The Ant has disappeared in the snow. The Grasshopper is found dead in a drug-related incident and the house, now abandoned, is taken over by a gang of spiders who terrorize the once peaceful neighborhood.

I couldn't believe that she sent this to me... at first I laughed. But after a while, the analogy started to get under my skin. I think it bothered me, because even though it was meant to be funny, the racial overtones were clear. It bothered me, because I had done everything in my power to dispel the myth that somehow all minorities were only interested in handouts and entitlements from the government. Certainly, in my experience, all of the blacks and Latinos I knew worked hard, had good jobs, and weren't on food stamps, unemployment, or any of the government handouts (except for the elderly who were on Social Security and/or Medicare).

So yes, I was offended, but only because this was a stereotypical narrative on minorities that I have seen continually played out over the years. I have to admit that even at the ripe old age of 40, I was a card carrying liberal. Like most liberals, I thought I knew so much more than those dyed-in-the-wool conservative Republicans. Heck, we liberals care about people, about the environment, about the sick, the poor, minorities, unions, and the wild-assed white bellied speckled chipmunks. What do Republicans care about? I used to believe that their only concern was to line the pockets of CEO's. I used to believe that Republicans ignored "we the people". All they cared about was developing and maintaining the corrupt symbiotic relationship between the politicians who legalize tax breaks for those evil special-interests corporations in exchange for campaign donations from those same special interests so that these politicians can remain in power, i.e., "I'll scratch your back if you'll scratch mine." As I will reveal later in this book, I was SOOO wrong. It's not limited to the Republicans.

I got my first real job when I was 14 years old. I worked for a custodial company as a janitor. This was not a pleasant job as I had to clean the bathroom stalls at truck stops. The smell of urine, vomit, and whatever else may have occurred the day before would greet me as I entered into the men's restroom. Sometimes I felt like a gas mask would have been a nice accessory for the job. Although the pay was only about $2.00 an hour, that was a pretty good wage for me back then... heck, at fourteen I had my own spending money. It became very easy for me to become a fiscal conservative because I could equate time to money. The more time I spent working, the more money I would have to spend. Anytime I wanted to purchase something,

I could relate it to how much time I would have to work to buy it. Credit wasn't an option. I would have to SAVE first, PURCHASE later. Wow, what an unusual concept. Any guess where we would be as a country if we followed those same principles today?

I eventually graduated from truck stops and moved up to department stores during the summer. One incident, which still remains with me today, occurred when a manager of a downtown store in Colorado Springs asked me to clean the circular air vents on the ceiling, as they were accumulating a lot of dust. Of course I obliged him, so I went to the storeroom and pulled out a twelve-foot ladder along with a dust mop so that I could reach the vents. While I was at the top of the ladder on my tippy toes so I could reach the air vents, I started knocking the dust off of the vents as requested. I shifted the ladder to the second vent, and as I was repeating what I had previously done, the store manager came running out of his office screaming at me red-faced. He looked up at me, pointed his finger and shouted "You stupid idiot, you are supposed to cover the clothes with plastic first!!" I was embarrassed and ashamed. He was right. I should have known to cover the clothes. I was fourteen.

Ok, I screwed up on that one, but it wasn't like it was a Neiman Marcus or Saks Fifth Avenue store. This place was selling women's tube tops and hot pants, for God's sake. At that point, I decided I would never, ever let anyone talk to me like that again. I also decided that I no longer wanted to be a janitor where someone could treat me that way. As stated previously, I was already motivated to do more with my life, but that one incident solidified for me a desire to get a good education. I knew, even at 14, that education was the key to upward mobility and I was determined to get there.

Despite my liberal bias leanings and my bleeding-heart for the downtrodden, my parents did instill in me a work ethic that remains with me today. I learned early on, that nothing is for free. If one wants something, whether it is a material belonging, or an aspiration for a particular career choice, or the pursuit of athletic excellence, it will take hard work on one's part. No one is going to "give you" what you want. People may assist you in your endeavor, but ultimately, you must put in the effort to achieve your goals in life. That is the simple truth.

Grasshopper's Perspective

Our email relationship began in earnest after our first meeting. 2004 was an election year and there were plenty of issues to debate and discuss. The first thing I sent Anthony was the Ant & the Grasshopper story, the moral of which if you work hard, you will have a roof over your head and food to eat, and if you don't, you won't. Well, that got Anthony's dander up, and he suggested we meet at Michael's again to discuss it further and to bring friends and family along. And so began what would become a weekly Thursday meeting of 6-8 people that discussed all things taboo: politics, religion, race and sex. This is also where the monikers Ant and Grasshopper began. How I became the grasshopper is beyond me, but I think it's because his name began with "Ant," and my name began with

"G." Our weekly meetings became affectionately known as the "Insect Club."

I remember when Bush won the election: I emailed Ant and said "I'm doing the happy dance!" I think I was happier to have beaten Ant than anything else. This was his email response —

Anthony's e-mail: November 9, 2004

Okay you two debutantes (he was responding to both RHB and me) enough is enough!! I concede that the Republicans won fair and square!! I agree that Kerry may not have been the best candidate this country has to offer up to challenge Bush, but unfortunately, individuals smart enough to run this country are also smart enough to avoid the political process required to get elected. So, we get people like "Bush" and "Kerry" to lead this country. Granted the Democrats need to reassess their views, lick their wounds, and find a moderate "centralist" candidate that better reflects the core of America.

I honestly don't believe that you all think that Bush is the best this country has to offer as a leader. I think you all were just anti-Kerry as much as I was anti-Bush. So be it - but it is incumbent upon us to do better as a united country to find leaders that try to bring us together and support our core beliefs and challenge us as a nation to do better. I'm not sure Bush will do that. What sacrifices has he asked us to make to support the war? None. The single most defining moment in his presidency, and he has yet to ask the American people to unite and sacrifice to support our troops. Rich or poor, black or white, east coast or west coast, liberal or conservative, we can all agree that the war and our security is the current issue, so use it to unite us in a common struggle and tell the American people the truth that sacrifices must be made at all levels (soldiers who give their life for their country give the ultimate sacrifice), and if we should have to pay more taxes to balance the budget and support our defense industry then so be it. Energy independence should be a cornerstone of our national security policy, or let's just get on with it and convert Iraq into the 51st state so that we own the oil and can become independent of the oil from Saudi Arabia and Iran - just a few crazy and random thoughts on my part.

Having said all of that... there are a few Republicans I would probably vote for president... John McCain, Colin Powell, Ashcroft (just kidding). Are there any Democrats you would consider for the presidency, or are you both ideologues?

Grasshopper's Response:

My answer to that was an emphatic "NO!" I didn't think I was an ideologue per se, but I knew I certainly was not a big government girl. I think that's why I like Texas. We breed independent thinkers and doers. People who are not from Texas just don't get Texans. I love Texas. It conjures up visions of proud, free and independent souls. My counter to those who do not like Texans and their love for Texas is to say "Just love YOUR state as much as we love Texas." Anthony, like most folks unfamiliar with the Lone Star state, had a misperception of what Texas was like, and especially what conservative Texas women were like. A sampling of some of his earlier emails to me reveals his biases (although in truth I believe most of what he said was merely to push my buttons):

Anthony's e-mail: February 2, 2005

By the way, I know who created guilt... the religious right and those stick-in-the-mud Stepford-wife-like Republican women. I know you agree.

Anthony's e-mail: March 24, 2005

Ok Grasshopper:

What is loud, proud, walks on a cloud and is full of crap? A TEXAN!! Ok, we can discuss at Michael's tonight! Invite the gang of Ladybug, Young Guy, June Bug, and Butterfly... yes, Butterfly. She has never gone out with us to see how crazy we really are!! You ARE the social coordinator. YOU ARE ALSO THE LIFE OF THE PARTY!! There is no party without you there!!

Anthony's e-mail: April 12, 2005

Now, do you see what I mean about Texas Republican women and the fact that the chips in their heads malfunction on a regular basis? When you hit "reply," do not hit "reply to all" or your return message will go to everyone. As a second check, you might want to look at the distribution list just to see whom it is going to before you hit the SEND BUTTON. Is that too much to ask? I understand that you Texas Republican women are brain dead, just pretty bodies, operating on batteries, with no central processing chips worth a damn in the head unit. I can't have a decent conversation with either of you that isn't all about Texas, or cowboys, or horses, or boots, or cattle, or oil, or Bush, or... you know, all that stuff you are programmed to spew out.

Tsk, tsk, tsk... this is what I'm dealing with. I would hate to see how you operate on a task more complicated than e-mail. Got your blood boiling yet?

Grasshopper's Thoughts:

I have to admit, he did get my blood boiling. I love a good fight and Ant gave me one. Geez, I used to get so mad at him, but always in a good way. He had a warped view about Texans and Republican women. However, in time, he became one of my most trusted friends. I couldn't wait for our "Insect Club" Thursday evening meetings as I was always up for a good debate. But alas, our time was short-lived. In the summer of 2005, Ant took a job in Albuquerque, New Mexico. It was a great move for him professionally, but one of my best friends was moving away. We stayed in touch, but he was gone. And my life was headed for a change.

In July of 2005, I separated from my husband on my 50th birthday and in August of 2005 my daddy had a heart attack and a subsequent quadruple heart bypass surgery that led to a massive stroke. It was heartbreaking. Not only was I mourning my marriage, I was mourning the loss of the daddy I once knew. My daddy passed away in January of 2006 and my marriage came to an end in May of 2006. That summer,

Ant invited me out to Albuquerque. Our relationship was easy. We picked right up where we did before. I remember when I first told my boss Shane that I was going out to Albuquerque to visit Ant, he was none too pleased. He just wasn't sure it was a good idea. I asked him if race had anything to do with it. He said no, but my gut told me yes. Shane knew Ant and thought he was a great guy, so why didn't he want me to go out there? Ant's race may have played a part of it, but Shane was protective of me. We had worked together for over 20 years. We were family, and after my divorce, he just wanted the best for me. He later told me he didn't want anyone saying anything bad about me because I was dating a black man. It wasn't that he minded, but he was concerned that others would treat me differently. My response to Shane was that if it bothered others that I was dating a black man, it was their problem. Why would I associate with them? Thankfully, none of my friends have abandoned me because of our interracial relationship.

In late summer of 2006, my three bosses knew Ant was coming into town and they decided they wanted to take him out to lunch. Ant was hesitant as he knew that they were protective of me. They went to pick him up at my house and Ant said if they had shown up in a pick-up truck wearing white hoods, he wasn't getting in the truck. Ha! Nonetheless, they took him to a local hamburger joint called Fred's. A greasy spoon sort of place with bosomy waitresses. During the lunch they talked about everything under the sun, what Ant does for a living, etc. Towards the end of the lunch, Ant brought up the elephant in the room. Ant, in a matter-of-fact tone, asked "So, I hear you all have a problem with my dating Glenna. Is it because I'm black?" You could have heard a pin drop. Giving credit to Shane, he stepped up while the other two, Fred and Mickey, remained quiet. Shane admitted that it surprised him that he cared about the black-white thing. His best friend in college, Jackson, was black. In fact, Jackson and Shane were the first interracial roommates at North Texas University. They both ran track. Jackson and Shane remain good friends even to today. For Shane, the thought that he had reservations about Ant because of his color was problematic. Shane freely admitted his concerns to Ant and recognized that he needed to look himself in the mirror regarding his attitude about Ant. Prior to ending the lunch with my three bosses, Ant asked them "Is Glenna happy?" They all had to admit that I was extremely happy. The funny thing is they all hold Ant in high esteem today. I learn every day it is not about color, it is about character. Color is irrelevant.

In December of 2006, I had a Christmas Party in Fort Worth, Texas to introduce my friends to Ant. Up to this point, I had mostly been traveling to Albuquerque and many of my friends had never seen me out with Ant. One of my friends, Porter, had no idea that Ant was black. So, in true Texas form, my boss Shane pointed to two men in the kitchen, and said to Porter who was standing next to him "There's the guy Glenna is dating!" Well, one of them was Ant and the other was a white friend of mine, who was sporting a new earring. Porter looked at Shane and said that he couldn't believe Glenna was dating a guy with an earring! Shane looked at Porter and said "You are looking at the wrong guy!" The thought that I would be dating Ant never crossed Porter's mind... funny how that works.

On April 12, 2008, I married an awesome man, who just happens to be black. I just happen to be white. The whole notion of our skin color sounds silly when put in print. Ant and I met during an election year and we got married in an election year. Still we were on different sides of the aisle politically. We were stuck on Republican versus Democrat, but as we would soon learn, the issues this country faces are much bigger than the political parties.

Chapter 2

THE AWAKENING

 Marriage. The ceremony where two people unite and bond together forever in the eyes of God. It's a very emotional commitment. I personally believe it is a commitment that can only be met if each person is allowed to grow at his or her own rate, and can bring what they have learned back into the relationship. If neither party grows, the relationship will wither.

Grasshopper and I do not have that problem. She is an incessant reader of books, novels, magazines, and Internet blogs. She has a voracious appetite for knowledge and an abundance of energy to feed that appetite. Me... I am more strategic. I ponder, and then I explain. Grasshopper may read something interesting and refer it to me. I will interpret and explain it back to her. We make a good team.

Banking 101

Imagine you are a banker. Let's assume you are the owner of Good Deal Bank. Like any banker, your job is to make a profit at the end of the year. How do you do that as a banker, who does nothing but holds other people's money? Like any business, you have got to convince people that for the privilege of holding onto their money, you will give them a little interest on the money they leave in your bank. So why would you pay people more money back then what they gave to you? That seems like a losing proposition. If everyone gives me their money, and I have to give them more money back at the end of the year – I'm losing money, right?

So, in order for me to make some money, I must take some of the deposits from the people who have given me their money on loan, and offer it up to other entities (individuals, small businesses, corporations) who need the capital to improve their livelihood (to buy a car, re-model a restaurant, purchase a new manufacturing plant). Of course, as the Good Deal banker, and because I'm taking a risk by lending you someone else's money, I intend to charge you a higher interest rate than I am paying my depositors. Of course, it is my responsibility to ensure that the folks I am lending money to be capable of paying me back. I better be darn sure my risk is small because it's not my money that I am lending out. So my profit is the difference between the interest I charge those to whom I've given a loan and the interest I must pay my depositors, minus my expenses (labor, taxes, maintenance, utilities, etc.).

Think about it. This is really a good deal for me the banker. I make money on other people's money and all I have to do is find credit-worthy folks to lend money to. Usually that is easy if I have good screening criteria: the borrower must have a job, limited expenses, and a history of steady income. Banking is easy.

Now, if I'm stupid enough to give money to someone I know is incapable of paying me back, whose fault is that? Mine. I know this first hand because I have done so on a number of occasions. I have given friends "interest-free loans" and to this day, I have not seen a return of my original loan. They know who they are, and they have somehow lost contact with me over the years. Finally, after being the bleeding-heart liberal turned "sucker" for the last time, I was approached by a friend who wanted to borrow some money and she asked me if I could help her out. This time, I told her that I would, but I would charge her interest. We had a written agreement, and I received monthly payments until the debt was eventually re-paid. She was grateful for the loan, and I was happy that I could help her out. You see, after losing my shirt a couple of times, I became a smarter banker. She and I are still friends to this day.

There are some people who might be offended that I would charge a friend interest on the use of my money. Why? If I just leave my money in the bank, the bank will pay me interest. So if I lend money to a friend, I have not only lost the use of the original dollars to purchase something for myself, but I have also lost the interest the bank was willing to pay me on that money. Hence, the interest I should charge my friend should cover both the interest I am losing from my local bank, but also the cost of the loss opportunity of money that isn't available to reinvest somewhere else. My word of advice, don't hesitate to charge your "needy" friends an interest rate commensurate with the risk they present - and get it in writing. If they are offended, so be it. It's probably a good indication that they had no intention of paying you back. They will have moved from the category of friend to moocher. Don't lend to moochers.

So as I said before, banking is easy as long as I do my one job very well, *i.e.,* screen the folks I lend money to. Well, most banks used to do that, and then we had the fiasco known as Fannie Mae (Federal National Mortgage Association) and Freddie Mac (Federal Home Loan Mortgage Corporation).

Let's go back in time to get a little historical perspective. The Boston Globe released an op-ed article written by Jeff Jacoby on September 28, 2008, which explains what happened:

> *"The roots of this [financial] crisis go back to the Carter administration. That was when government officials, egged on by left-wing activists, began accusing mortgage lenders of racism and "redlining" because urban blacks were being denied mortgages at a higher rate than suburban whites.*
>
> *The pressure to make more loans to minorities (read: to borrowers with weak credit histories) became relentless. Congress passed the Community Reinvestment Act; empowering regulators to punish banks that failed to "meet the credit needs" of "low-income, minority, and distressed neighborhoods." Lenders responded by loosening their underwriting standards and making increasingly shoddy loans. The two government-chartered mortgage finance firms, Fannie Mae and Freddie Mac, encouraged*

this "subprime" lending by authorizing ever more "flexible" criteria by which high-risk borrowers could be qualified for home loans, and then buying up the questionable mortgages that ensued.

All this was justified as a means of increasing homeownership among minorities and the poor. Affirmative-action policies trumped sound business practices. A manual issued by the Federal Reserve Bank of Boston advised mortgage lenders to disregard financial common sense. "Lack of credit history should not be seen as a negative factor," the Fed's guidelines instructed. Lenders were directed to accept welfare payments and unemployment benefits as 'valid income sources' to qualify for a mortgage. Failure to comply could mean a lawsuit." [Jacoby, 2008].

It is easy to be a banker until a government regulator threatens you with a lawsuit requiring you to give loans to people who don't meet your financial standards. In order to keep the Feds at bay, you, Mr. Banker, must provide for the downtrodden so that they too can live in a house. Many private banks got out of the business to protect their depositors; however, Fannie and Freddie dove head first into the loan business by buying and packaging these mortgages. Hence, the private banks and mortgage companies were no longer concerned about liability, as long as they did as the government regulators directed and could sell their loans to Fannie & Freddie.

In 2008, when it became obvious that many of the lower-income clients were defaulting on their loans due to loss of income, loss of a job, unable to make balloon payments, etc., Fannie and Freddie were left holding the bag. Now, who is at fault - the banker for giving out the loans or the government for coercing the banker to give out the loans to less than credit-worthy clients? Both.

Back in 2008, even with my liberal biases at the time, I felt that there should be consequences for bad behavior. Fannie and Freddie were supposedly Government Sponsored Enterprises (GSE's) that were privately owned. They made a number of bad decisions and instead of allowing the consequences of those decisions to fall squarely on the bankers, our government in the form of the U.S. Treasury came to the rescue and bailed them out. Who is now paying for those defaulted mortgages? We the taxpayers. As of May 2012, Fannie and Freddie are still bleeding money even after the taxpayers have provided them over $150 billion in bailout funds. This is happening because property values continue to drop, homeowners are defaulting in droves, and because of the guarantees on the loans, Fannie and Freddie must pay for the losses!

The U.S. Treasury doesn't have any money. They get their money by taxing the rest of us. Is that fair? Something didn't smell right to me. Rule #3. *If it doesn't smell right, it ain't right.* I decided to follow my nose.

The Baddest Bank Around

Clearly, something had run amok during the financial crisis of 2008. Right before the election of Barack Obama,

President Bush signed the Troubled Asset Relief Program (TARP) bill into law on October 3, 2008. It allowed the U.S. Treasury to purchase up to $700B in financial assets from the bank and mortgage industries. It ticked me off. It seemed to go against everything I believed about the free enterprise system and it also appeared to reward those who were reckless (those greedy millionaire and billionaire bankers). Heck, if I loaned out other people's money, collected interest on that money from my client, and then if my client turned out to be a bad risk and decided he was no longer going to pay me back, normally I would have to suck it up and absorb the loss. Bankers don't think like you and me. They want to eliminate all risk, so what do they do next? Instead of "breaking the kneecaps" of the guy who won't pay the loan back (are Chicago mobsters still doing that?), the bankers cut a deal with our government, the U.S. Treasury to guarantee them the money owed to them by the deadbeat, if he defaults.

Remember, all you have to do to be a Good Deal Banker is identify credit worthy clients. Now, if the government is going to bail me out if I screw up, I don't really have to work that hard. I just need to find people who want to borrow my money (oops, I mean YOUR money), and if they don't pay me back, the U.S. Treasury will pay me back! Sweeeeet! Now here is the funny thing, the U.S. Treasury gets its money by taxing YOU!

This banking stuff is getting easier. I use your money to make me money. If I screw up, and the people I gave your money to don't pay me back, then I go to the agency that already took your money through taxes and I ask them to pay me back the money you loaned to me in the first place so the money you originally deposited is still there. Wow! The taxpayer takes all the risks, and the banker gets all of the rewards. Everybody should want to be a banker!

Maybe it's coincidental, but I have always believed that if you need something in your life, God will place opportunities in front of you to help you achieve your goals. It is still up to you individually to take advantage of the opportunity, but you have to be mentally and spiritually ready to recognize the opportunity in front of you and realize that it aligns with your goals.

If I really wanted to understand the 2008 fiscal crisis, I felt I needed to understand banks. Well, it just so happens, that my wife's boss, Shane, had recently come across a book entitled *The Creature from Jekyll Island* written by G. Edward Griffin [Griffin, 2002]. The book inspired Shane and he felt that it was important enough to buy a number of these books to distribute to everyone in his office. Of course, Grasshopper brought it home to me and said I should read it. I was reluctant at first because when I saw the tag line: *A Second Look at the Federal Reserve.* I thought to myself... BORING! Who reads this stuff?

So I sat down and skimmed through the Table of Contents and read the Foreword. It intrigued me. This was a story about money, how it works, why it works, who makes it, and how bankers and politicians manipulate it. So, I started to read, and then I read some more, and some more, and I became absolutely engrossed in the storyline. The first 100 pages blew me away! Why wasn't I taught this in school? All of a sudden, my entire worldview began to change as I read through this history lesson on the creation of the Federal Reserve. This was NOT boring. This book opened my eyes to how the current system works, and I could see it being played out in real time during the 2008 fiscal crisis.

Presently, I completely understand that the system is rigged and that politicians and bankers will do EVERYTHING and ANYTHING to remain in power, even at the expense of "we the taxpayers." Let me see if I can summarize in a few paragraphs what G. Edward Griffin did in his well-researched reference guide.

First, the Federal Reserve is NOT a federal entity. It is no more a federal agency than FedEx or Apple Computer. The Federal Reserve is a privately owned cartel of bankers established in 1913 as the nation's central banking system. Unlike a regular bank, where you must attract depositors, the Federal Reserve has built-in depositors. They divided the U.S. into 12 Districts and require the member banks from each of the 12 districts to deposit their reserve accounts into the system. If one bank goes south due to a screw-up, the Federal Reserve can move money around in these Districts to shore up the accounts in banks where things went bad, thereby maintaining the integrity of the banking system. This sounded pretty good to me. What was Rule number 2: *Don't believe everything you hear, because your ears will lie to you.*

Let's be clear, first and foremost, the Federal Reserve is composed of bankers. We know bankers make money on other people's money. In the case of the Federal Reserve, their main client is the U.S. Treasury. The Federal Reserve lends money to the U.S. Treasury. The U.S. Treasury in return, must pay back the Federal Reserve with interest. Who does the U.S. Treasury represent? It represents us, the taxpayers. So, the Federal Reserve lends money to our government (U.S. Treasury), who in turn, can confiscate it from us in the form of additional taxes.

Let's say the U.S. Treasury needs to borrow more money from the Fed to pay for all of those federal agencies like the Department of Energy, the Department of Education, the Environmental Protection Agency, etc. Typically, the U.S. Treasury would offer a bond to individuals and foreign governments in return for their depositing cash with the U.S. Treasury today. The bond is simply an IOU to the folks that lend their money to the U.S. Treasury. It's a promise to pay them back over a certain period of time with a given interest rate. Remember the old Popeye cartoons and the chubby character Wimpy who said "I will gladly pay you Tuesday for a hamburger today." Our U.S. Treasury is Wimpy on steroids. They will gladly pay you later, if you feed the Beast (our government) now.

The U.S. Treasury funds the government, and right now our U.S. Treasury must borrow 40 cents for every dollar that it spends. In other words, the revenue that the U.S. Treasury is taking in through taxes is insufficient to fund the government we have created. Our government must borrow the rest. The U.S. Treasury does this through "bond auctions." Unfortunately for the U.S. Treasury, foreign governments are catching on and are no longer willing to subsidize our spending habits by buying our bonds at these auctions. Especially, since we are offering such low interest rates to anyone stupid enough to lend money to the U.S.

So, if our Treasury needs more money, and individuals and foreign governments are no longer willing to lend their money to us... who will? The Federal Reserve. Those bankers who are in the Federal Reserve cartel are willing to lend money to the U.S. Treasury for a lower-than-market interest rate.

Here is the kicker, and this is what makes the Federal Reserve the baddest bank around. As we stated before, bankers don't like to use their own money. They will NEVER, NEVER, NEVER ever risk their own money. The Federal Reserve doesn't have enough money to continually fund the U.S. Treasury's appetite for more cash. So, what do they do? The U.S. Treasury auctions a bond to the Federal Reserve. The Federal Reserve buys the bond (SINCE IT IS GUARANTEED BY THE U.S. GOVERNMENT) and deposits a few hundred billion dollars into the U.S. Treasury account for them to use to meet expenses. Where did this money come from? Nowhere! Those dollars appeared out of thin air in an electronic banking account for the U.S. Treasury to feed the Beast and keep the doors open in the government.

Of course, the U.S. Treasury (we the taxpayers) are now on the hook to repay that bond with interest to the Federal Reserve (the banking cartel). Geez - it doesn't get any better than this - the Fed bankers create money out of thin air and get us the taxpayer to pay it back to them WITH INTEREST. I can just hear those Federal Reserve bankers talking amongst themselves when referring to the masses "YOU SUCKERS ALL WORK FOR US NOW!"

The Rest of the Story

So what does this all mean? Who cares that money is created out of thin air? Remember, money is a representation of one's work. It has value, because it represents your time, your energy, and your creativity. If someone can create money out of thin air, then it devalues the currency. No effort is required. Ah, a light bulb just went on in my head. It is starting to make sense to me why the Founding Father's stated that only Congress shall have the power to coin money and fix the standards of Weights and Measures. Note the Constitution stated very clearly that Congress shall have the power, NOT the Federal Reserve. Back then, the federal currency was only gold and silver coins. That is because it takes WORK to get the metal out of the ground, to refine and purify it, and to coin it. The work required to create the coins is what gives them their value.

The original intent of the Federal Reserve was to maintain a stable currency. This means that as the population grows and productivity increases, the amount of currency in distribution should be controlled to ensure that the purchasing power of the currency remains flat or stable. Think about what that means. Is the purchasing power of a dollar in 1913 when the Fed was created equivalent to the purchasing power of a dollar today? Of course not, because the Federal Reserve has NOT done what it agreed to do. It has been an absolute failure. Prior to 1913, the U.S. currency was stable. According to the Bureau of Labor Statistics own website, the purchasing power of a dollar in 1913 is equivalent to $23.17 in 2012. This means that the dollars you saved earlier in your life are worth less today. Since 1913, the dollar has lost more than 95% of its value! The Federal Reserve, by printing dollars out of thin air, is quietly stealing from your bank account by devaluing the dollars you have already saved. Inflation, typically manifested in higher prices for everything, is not NORMAL. The Fed wants us to believe that inflation is normal, so that the elite few bankers, who can literally print money out of thin air, can use the funds to do whatever they need... pay back loans that went bad, influence politicians, make deals with corporations, etc. The Federal Reserve is the source of all the distortions, booms, and busts in the market place.

Another way to look at this is through the principle of dilution. Assume you have a glass of wine that is half full. Let's assume it's a really good glass of red wine called Chateau L 'Expensive Rouge. One can imagine the work that went into creating this wine, the planting of the seeds, the watering, the harvesting of the grapes, the monitoring in the barrels, and finally the bottling. Now what if someone came along and decided to add some more wine to your glass. Except, all they were really adding is a little bit of water. At first you might not notice, but then they add a little more water, and then a little more water, and then a little more water. At some point, Chateau L 'Expensive

Rouge becomes John Stewart's Pink Ripple! The wine has been diluted and what remains is no longer worth the price of the original. By printing money out of thin air, the Federal Reserve is diluting and devaluing the money supply we have already earned. This is why everything is getting more expensive. A dollar in the year 2000 had the purchasing power of $1.33 today. The Fed is stealing from all of us and will continue to do so. Why? Because they are bankers - it's what they do. Our politicians allow them to do it. Why? Because they want to continue to spend money in their districts for YOUR vote. Everyone wins except "we the people" and the generations to follow after us. If you don't understand this, then nothing else in this book will make sense to you. If this resonates with you, then you are on the road to reality. If not, go back and read this section again!

My Alarm is Ringing

The sudden knowledge about how the banking system works and how the system is rigged to protect the banks and keep the politicians in power was a rude awakening for me. All of a sudden, the old debates of Democrat versus Republican became nonsensical to me - both are merely two sides of the same coin - so I thought.

In early 2009, I started to wake up. I wanted to learn more and began reading other books. I read Mark Levin's *Liberty and Tyranny: A Conservative Manifesto* [Levin, 2009], followed by W. Cleon Skousen's *The Five*

Thousand Year Leap: 28 Great Ideas That Changed the World [Skousen, 2009]. These books opened my eyes to the lies and deceptions perpetrated by the Progressives who have infiltrated our educational, government, media, and judicial institutions. The light bulb came on, and it became clear that I could no longer support any form of liberalism, even in its renamed form of progressivism, socialism, communism, and totalitarianism. The former eventually leads to the latter. History shows this to always be true.

Prior to 2009, I had never heard of Glenn Beck. I didn't know who he was, what he did, or his history. However, my wife and I began recording his show on the FOX News channel because it seemed intriguing. Who was this wacky guy on at 3 pm MST scribbling on a chalkboard, connecting the dots between politicians, corporations, media outlets, and elite financiers? Who was this guy willing to take the Obama Administration head-on and link Obama to a web of avowed socialists and communists in his administration? People like: Van Jones, former Green Jobs Czar; Communist Mao-Loving Anita Dunn; White House Communications Director Valerie Jarrett, Assistant to the President and daughter-in-law to Vernon Jarrett an avowed communist; socialist Carol Browner, dumped as Climate Czar; Ron Bloom, Senior Counselor to the U.S. President for Manufacturing Policy who stated in 2008, "We know that the free market is nonsense. We kind of agree with Mao that political power comes largely from the barrel of a gun."; Regulatory Affairs Czar, Cass "Nudge 'em" Sunstein; Elizabeth "I am Cherokee Tomahawk Wampum" Warren, former communist head of the Consumer Financial Bureau and newly-elected 2012 Senator for Massachusetts; and FCC Diversity Czar, Mark Lloyd.

Most people have never heard of these folks. It's a shame that the mainstream media (MSM) refuses to shed light on these individuals who surround this president. Glenn Beck's staff always backed their allegations with videotapes of these individuals speaking in their own words. They always had proof.

How many socialist / communist sympathizers do you personally know? I don't know any, but I am starting to have some concern about a few of my liberal friends. Glenn Beck "outed" all of these people in Obama's Administration. There are probably many more still buried in the bowels of the executive branch. You can tell a lot about someone by the company they keep. Obama's associations are NOT normal. How could we as a nation allow this to happen in our country? Beck knew, like most people NOW know, that something didn't smell right in the MAObama Administration. Beck was right.

Interestingly, Glenn Beck always took the Progressives at their word. Because he could connect the dots, he would make predictions based on their own words. Here we are today, and every major prediction that Glenn Beck espoused has come true. I don't see anyone in the MSM doing any fact checking to show how accurate Mr. Beck was in 2009 and 2010. No. It's much easier to humiliate, criticize and deride him as some fringe lunatic. Trust me, Glenn Beck is no lunatic. I suggest to anyone who hears those types of comments to simply do their own homework and review his many forecasts and compare them to where we are today as a nation. You don't have to be Johnny Carson's Kreskin to figure this stuff out. All you have to do is take the Progressives (socialists/communists) at their word and listen.

I began watching Beck's show in earnest in early 2009 (and continue to on his Internet GBTV channel). All of a sudden, I became aware of a whole new perspective from which I had never viewed the world. It's akin to a fish that has lived in water its entire life, being snared out of a lake by a fisherman. Suddenly, this fish sees the water below it, a sky above it, and the shore to its side and the fish realizes that his reality is not THE reality. Seeing the world with this new perspective made me realize I could never go back in the water. I wanted to learn more, know more, and understand more about how the world really works.

I continued to educate myself by reading incessantly. Ron Paul's *End the Fed* [Paul, 2009] book makes a strong case to eliminate the Federal Reserve. I followed up by reading Thomas E. Woods Jr.'s book called *Meltdown: A Free-Market Look at Why the Stock Market Collapsed, the Economy Tanked, and Government Bailouts Will Make Things Worse* [Woods, 2009]. In *Meltdown,* Woods points out in Chapter 4 how the government causes the boom-bust business cycle. At this point, I started to get more resentful of the government-caused financial crisis. More recently, I obtained from Grasshopper a signed copy of the book *Aftershock: Protect Yourself and Profit in the Next Global Financial Meltdown* written by David Wiedemer [Wiedemer, 2011]. That title alone should give you pause...

yes, there will be another global financial meltdown. At the time of this writing, all indications suggest it will begin with the fragile European economy (i.e., the PIIGS - Portugal, Italy, Ireland, Greece, and Spain).

Grasshopper and I became more involved in the local Tea Party movement and started to meet similarly concerned citizens who were paying attention to the events of the day. I became active in getting the word out to people. I thought it would be a good thing to wake others up, to let them know there is a different world out there. All I have to do is get them to jump out of the water long enough to notice. Unfortunately, most people, like most fish, will never see beyond the water. It is what sustains and supports them.

I started my own YouTube channel (AntTV) [Thornton, 2011] and began creating YouTube videos so that I could share my new learning with others. My very first video nearly went viral as it reached over 330,000 views and was featured on Breitbart-tv.com. However, I was a novice to the whole YouTube process and because I utilized copyrighted music, YouTube's internal policies shut me down as the video was gaining steam. While I have no proof, I suspect the liberal media complained before it went viral nationally. Do I think that the Left would go out of its way to use copyright laws to shut down free speech? I don't know. Without proof, it would only be speculation. What do you think?

I am now reading Ayn Rand's *Atlas Shrugged* [Rand, 1957]. This is a great novel. I now understand why the book is not touted by the Progressives nor taught in schools. This novel highlights every tactic that the Progressives will use to create their utopian socialistic society. The novel highlights the collusion between the politicians and the mega-corporations that we see being played out in today's headlines.

Let me point out one example just to prove my case. Jon Corzine served in the United States Senate from 2001 to 2006 and then became the governor of New Jersey from 2006 through 2010. Prior to entering public life, he spent a majority of his career at Goldman Sachs where he had become chairman and senior partner. Hmmm - what does that make Mr. Corzine? He is fundamentally a banker. Remember, bankers don't think like the rest of us.

Jon Corzine is now the exiled chairman and chief executive officer of MF Global Holdings Inc., a failed brokerage firm. He resigned his position on November 4, 2011 under suspicion that he and other officers of the firm had taken some risks on high- interest rate European government bonds. When these bonds began losing value, MF Global had to declare bankruptcy. However, prior to the bankruptcy, $1.6 billion of clients' funds had been confiscated out of their accounts illegally in an attempt to save the firm. A single $175 million transfer occurred from a customer's account three days prior to the bankruptcy declaration which may have violated Security and Exchange Commission dictates according to a March 29, 2012 *Wall Street Journal* report.

Think about this for two seconds. Bankers don't like to take risks with their own money, but will with other people's money. Let's assume that MF Global made a bad bet, and was losing money. Maybe, due to regulations requiring a certain amount of reserve assets, MF Global had to "borrow" funds from their clients' accounts in order to shore up their own. Maybe, just maybe these elite financial geniuses were arrogant enough to believe that their European bond position was correct and that the market would turn around in their favor allowing them to pay back the borrowed money before their clients realized it had been confiscated. Clearly, their strategy failed. The firm declared bankruptcy on October 31, 2011 and their customers were left holding the bag. As of May 2012, no criminal charges have been brought against the executives of MF Global, including Jon Corzine. They have gotten away with robbery. Somehow, we are supposed to believe that this money simply disappeared as a result of a clerical error during the last few hectic hours of the firm's existence. Remember how bankers think: they will always get paid regardless of the risk. I guess those customers who were ripped off know what the MF stands for.

Here's a question for everyone. Why isn't someone in jail for stealing $1.6 billion? I realize that this isn't quite up to Bernie Madoff thievery standards, but why hasn't someone been prosecuted? Is it because Jon Corzine was a key supporter of Obama during his first election campaign? Is it because he is a major fundraiser and money bundler for the Obama campaign? Jon Corzine appears on the roster of Obama's 2012 Volunteer Fundraisers in the $500,000+ category. Maybe, just maybe if you can raise more than half a million dollars for the President's campaign, it won't matter that you stole a billion from unsuspecting clients. I don't know about you, but it doesn't smell right. You be the judge.

Chapter 3

1. **Facts have no bearing on the decision making process of the Progressive class.**

2. **America has a debt problem and a failure of leadership.**

Logic requires the ability to reason. Reason requires an ability to discern facts from fiction. I have come to the conclusion that facts, i.e., information that actually exists, information that is known to exist, information that is truthful and represents reality, has absolutely no bearing on the decision-making process of the Progressive class. Statists, socialists, and Marxists are nothing more than creatures of emotion that react spontaneously to the immediate stimulus in front of them rather than use any semblance of conscious mental effort. I'm not kidding. This is not hyperbole. Progressives are like children. They want gratification now, and they want gratification forever. Damn the facts.

The Facts

At the time of this writing, the following information on Obama's legacy since the day he took office is clear:

	January 2009	Today	% Change	Source
Avg. retail price/gallon gas in U.S.	$1.83	$3.63	+98.3%	U.S. Energy Information Administration
Sugar Cane, raw, world	$13.37	$20.84	+55.8%	ICE Futures, 6/15/2012
Unemployment Rate, Blacks	14.8%	15.8%	+6.7%	Bureau of Labor Statistics
Unemployment Rate, Overall	7.8%	8.2%	+3.7%	Bureau of Labor Statistics
Food Stamp Recipients	31.9 million	43.2 million	+35.1%	Supplemental Nutrition Assistance Program
National Debt ($ Trillions)	$10.627	$15.733	+48%	U.S. Debt Clock
People in Poverty, U.S.	39.8 million	43.6 million	+9.5%	U.S. Dept. of Agriculture

By any statistical standard, Obama's administration has failed to improve the economy. Energy and food prices are increasing, along with unemployment and food stamp recipients. In addition, his policies have had a more devastating impact on the poor and minority communities for whom he touts caring so much. Poppycock! Yes I said it, poppycock! Obama and his socialist ilk are dummies when it comes to economics. However, if you think like a socialist, you really do want more people dependent on the government. By socialist standards, Obama is an absolutely fantastic, overwhelming success! The more people he can make dependent on the government for their well-being, the more entitlements he can dispense to his supporters, the more government takeovers he can manipulate over private enterprises and the more money he can extract from the successful, then the more power he and the Progressive elite can wield against the U.S. populace. This is ultimately what he seeks, and this is what he meant when he said right before the 2008 election, "We are five days away from fundamentally transforming the United States of America!"

Obviously, none of this matters to Progressives. Consider the national debt numbers in the previous table. In Obama's first three and a half years since he took the office of the presidency, his policies have increased the national debt by more than $5.1 trillion dollars! This is nearly a trillion dollars more than the total accumulated debt of $4.16 trillion by all 41 U.S. presidents from George Washington through George H.W. Bush combined!

Obama is a spending machine. He is like some wild-eyed, drug-crazed, sugar-ladened, under-aged teenager running around with his parents' credit card buying up everything he can for himself and his friends. Consequences are meaningless to him. "Let's keep partying until my parents come home!" yells the teenager. All of his friends scream in delight as they trash the house leaving pizza and beer stains in every corner of the home. Obama, like the teenager, knows that eventually the parents will come home and there will be consequences for his behavior. But hey, there are no adults in the home for now, so let's keep this party going!

President Obama didn't even address the issue of the approaching debt crisis during his second term election campaign. He is a coward. He is a child. He needs parental guidance. Unfortunately, he isn't getting it from our so-called Republican representatives. They seem to have joined the party along with their Democratic brethren and continue extending the credit card limit every time Congress reaches a debt limit. Debt limit? What a joke - John Boehner and Mitch "Turtle-face" McConnell have done nothing to challenge this President's spending spree. They have led the Republican Party during the greatest government expansion and debt accrual since Herbert Hoover and the Great Depression. Oh sure, they whine and offer up proposals that claim to cut spending, but every time we as a nation approach the debt limit, they cave - every time.

So what is a trillion dollars? To most people these numbers are meaningless. If I were to convert dollars into seconds, it might become more meaningful to most people. Suppose I were to sit across a table from you and promise you a trillion dollars by handing you a dollar per second. Sixteen minutes and 40 seconds later you will have received $1000 from me. Not bad. After 11 days 13 hours 46 minutes and 40 seconds, you will have $1 million dollars on the table. I'll bet you are starting to get the hang of this, but we still have a long way to go. Now that you have your first million on the table, how long will it take for you to become a billionaire? In this case, we must assume that there are 365.25 days in a year (this takes into account that we have a leap day every four years). As we sit at the table, you will become a billionaire exactly 31 years 251 days 7 hours 46 minutes and 40 seconds after we started counting. Hmmm, that was a long time. However, I promised to give you a trillion dollars, right? Unfortunately, you will never get the trillion dollars from me, because we will both be dead long before we would reach that milestone. It would take me 31,688 years 32 days 1 hour 46 minutes and 40 seconds for us to exchange a trillion dollars! Amazing, huh? Maybe now, you understand what our government is doing to us.

It appears to me that the goal of the Progressive movement is to make more people dependent on the government. According to a recent Rasmussen survey [Rasmussen, 2012]:

"Most of the 46 million Americans living below the poverty level have adequate food, and three-quarters of them have a motor vehicle, according to federal household consumption surveys collected by pollster Scott Rasmussen.

Among Rasmussen's findings, reported by The Washington Examiner: 74 percent of the poor own a car or truck; 70 percent have a VCR; 64 percent have a DVD player; 63 percent have cable or satellite TV; 53 percent have a video game system; 50 percent have a computer; 30 percent have two or more cars; and 23 percent use TiVo."

Annual earnings of $22,314 are considered the 2010 poverty level for a family of four. Hence, America's poor is nowhere close to the poor of Africa, China, India, or the Middle East; however, Barack Obama has increased the number of poor in this nation. He is building his constituency.

In 2006, Senator Barack Hussein Obama commented on his predecessor George W. Bush's lack of leadership when Bush wanted to raise the debt ceiling. Obama's words were:

"The fact that we are here today to debate raising America's debt limit is a sign of leadership failure. It is a sign that the U.S. Government can't pay its own bills...Instead of reducing the deficit, as some people claimed, the fiscal policies of this administration and its allies in Congress will add more than $600 million in debt for each of the next five years...Increasing America's debt weakens us domestically and internationally. Leadership means that 'the buck stops here.' Instead, Washington is shifting the burden of bad choices today onto the backs of our children and grandchildren. America

has a debt problem and a failure of leadership. Americans deserve better."

Barack Obama stated in a 2009 interview with Matt Lauer

"...I will be held accountable. I've got four years. A year from now, I think people are going to see that we are starting to make some progress, but there is still going to be some pain out there. If I don't have this done in three years, then this is going to be a one-term proposition."

This man has never spoken truer words. Barack, in his own words and by his own standards has shown us his "failure of leadership." I hope Americans agree with him. I know the Progressives don't care, facts mean nothing to them.

Chapter 4

THE HYPOCRISY OF PROGRESSIVES

1. **99.9% of Americans are hypocrites.**

2. **Although we are all guilty, Progressives are worse than others.**

The interesting thing about hypocrisy is that 99.9% of us are hypocrites. According to the definition, a hypocrite is "a person who pretends to have virtues, moral, or religious beliefs, principles, etc. that he or she does not actually possess, especially a person whose actions belie stated beliefs." Listen, I hate calling everyone a hypocrite, but the truth is we are all flawed in some manner. You may support the "green agenda" and yet not recycle all of your trash. You may believe in global warming, but drive to work daily, fly in airplanes for business, and use electricity in your home from a coal burning plant. You may believe that everyone in this world can live in peace and harmony, while vilifying those filthy, racist bastards who disagree with you... hypocrite.

Hollywood

Hollywood directors, producers, actors and actresses comprise one of the most liberal groups in America. Did I really have to state that in print? Except for a few cases, most people in Hollywood are liberal... really? Some of the notable exceptions that come to mind include: Gary Sinise, Clint Eastwood, Sela Ward, Janine Turner, Dennis

Miller, Jon Voight, and most recently Jon Lovitz (by default of his recent tirade against Obama, he finally gets it). While I don't believe that a blacklist exists limiting the opportunities for these actors and comedians, my guess is that the number of scripts, roles, and opportunities for conservatives are extremely limited.

Personally, I don't know anyone who is "famous." I mean famous in the paparazzi sense that they are recognizable by face by the general public. While I hate to stereotype (but I will just to show what a hypocrite I am), I must admit that the majority of Hollywood types are blubbering idiots. Let's make a list of some of them... no on second thought, I've decided that would take up the remainder of this book and all we really need are a few examples.

Janeane Garofalo is the perfect case to examine Hollywood idiocy. I could have just as easily picked out Rosie O'Donnell, Susan Sarandon, Michael Moore, Eva Longoria, etc. but you will get the point. In response to the multitude of TEA Party protests around the nation, Janeane Garofalo was quoted as saying:

> "Let's be very honest about what this is about. It's not about bashing Democrats, it's not about taxes, they have no idea what the Boston tea party was about, they don't know their history at all. This is about hating a black man in the White House. This is racism straight up."

Really now? Well, according to the insightful and exquisitely informed Ms. Garofalo, not only is my wife a racist, so am I.

All of us TEA Party-types just hate to see a black man in the White House - really? Well, of course, that is what a liberal might think. Why else would we call it the White House? Up until Barack's election, the residence on Pennsylvania Avenue had only been inhabited by white folks and I guess the implication is that those TEA Party, red-neck, white supremacists are upset that the apple cart has been turned upside down by allowing a black man in the White House. However, those same racist TEA Party types supported Congressman Tim Scott (now Senator) in South Carolina and Allen West in Florida (don't look J-Garf, but they are both black Republicans), Nikki Haley in South Carolina (the daughter of Indian immigrants who were Sikhs), Susanna Martinez in New Mexico (the first female Hispanic governor of New Mexico), and of course, Marco Rubio in Florida (born to Cuban immigrants). Ms. Garofalo, don't you hate it when you can't pin down "those" TEA Party people by putting them in a little box and labeling it RACISTS?

Here is another quote from J-Garf:

> *"When I see the American flag, I go, 'Oh my God, you're insulting me.' "*

Need we say any more about J-Garf's worldview? I would like to see her go to one of her favored countries (maybe somewhere like Iran or Saudi Arabia) and see how far she can get away with that type of inflammatory speech about THEIR flag.

Clearly, Ms. Garofalo has never been to a TEA Party event. I have personally attended several and each time I have been treated not only with respect, but those in attendance have warmly welcomed me. Ms. Garofalo obviously has no knowledge or respect for the intent of the Founding Fathers in writing the Declaration of Independence and the Constitution. I find it curious that the Progressives get so riled up whenever you mention either document in their presence. Try it and watch their reaction... you will smile with glee as they twist themselves in knots over talk of the Constitution. When they scream... "it's about a woman's right for contraception," or "everyone has a right to a college education," or "everyone deserves a home," or "everyone has a right to decent medical care," etc., it's clear to me that they haven't a clue what an "inalienable right" really is as written in the Deck-of-I (that's my new pet phrase for the Declaration of Independence).

I like to ask liberals, "where do rights come from?" Sadly, most of them answer that our rights come from the government. Idiots. If someone has to pay for something, then it isn't a right! Whenever the Left claims something is a "right," I always ask "at whose expense?" If I have to pay for someone else's "right," then that makes me their slave. Think about it... if **I'M** working to pay for something **YOU** want or need, doesn't that make me your slave? My time and labor pays for your contraception... hmm, since I personally don't need any contraception, I must be working for you. Wow, most liberals don't look at themselves as plantation owners. "Liberals ARE," as J-Garf might say, "straight up slave owners!!" This is what the liberal agenda is all about. Of course, most children who want something don't look at it this way either. Liberals only know what they want, and if someone else must pay for it, who cares? It's not their money. Note to the working class: "Don't let these power hungry, Progressive slave owners get anywhere near your pocketbook!"

Most of the time Liberals are clueless because they have never read the founding documents themselves. Those that have read the documents, like our President Barack Obama, totally misinterpret the meaning of the documents (intentionally in my humble opinion) to make their case. In an interview as state Senator on Chicago's public radio station WBEZ-FM, Obama stated in 2001 that he believed the Warren Court's decisions on civil rights in the 1960s failed to go far enough and that they should have sought "redistributive justice." Here was his quote taken from that interview:

"...the Supreme Court never ventured into the issues of redistribution of wealth, and of more basic issues such as political and economic justice in society. To that extent, as radical as I think people try to characterize the Warren Court, it wasn't that radical. It didn't break free from the essential constraints that were placed by the Founding Fathers in the Constitution, at least as it's been interpreted, and the Warren Court interpreted in the same way, that generally the Constitution is a charter of negative liberties. Says what the states can't do to you. Says what the federal government can't do to you, but doesn't say what the federal government or state government must do on your behalf."

President Obama is absolutely correct. The Deck-of-I and the Constitution do not say what the government must do on our behalf other than to protect our individual rights. That's it. My crazy wife Grasshopper always ends her email with the following quote from Thomas Jefferson:

The two enemies of the people are criminals and government, so let us tie the second down with the chains of the Constitution so the second will not become the legalized version of the first.

This is the essential battle of our day. Whether we allow our government to tell us what we can and cannot do on "our behalf." The Constitution is pretty clear on this issue... a person would only see it as a charter of "negative liberties" if they felt constrained by its directives. If you are for an all-powerful government, you would hate the Constitution because it prevents you from acting like a king or dictator. Guess who hates the Constitution? Progressives and our President. What do you think they seek? More control, more power, more intrusion into our daily lives. Look at "Nanny" Mayor Bloomberg. First, there is a ban on cigarettes (on our behalf), then a citywide ban on salt (on our behalf), and now he's banning the size of my "Big Gulp" cup (on our behalf). This is just the beginning folks, I don't think it will stop there. Bloomberg is a "straight-up tyrant." Don't you just love that J-Garf expression? What gives HIM the right to tell me what to put in MY belly?

I always thought it was strange that liberals are quick to call conservatives (who want less government intrusion)

Nazis and tyrants. The truth is, these Progressives won't stop until they create this Utopian vision where everyone's daily actions are controlled by the state. Orwell's 1984 is quickly approaching and unless we stand and fight back, the Progressives may succeed.

Then we have our favorite atheist, misogynist, television host Bill Maher. Notice, I didn't describe him as a stand-up comedian, mainly because to obtain that descriptor, a prerequisite is that you have to be funny. He isn't funny. I personally like using the term misogynist... it makes me sound like a liberal ... we know how Progressives like labeling people. Now William "Misogynist" Maher Jr. is himself a hypocrite. He's ready to stand up for a woman's right to kill babies (we will talk about abortion a little later in this chapter), while at the same time calling Governor Sarah Palin a "c**t" and a "dumb twat." Wow, excuse me, but where does the National Organization for Women (N.O.W.) stand on this? Let me be clear for just one second... let's replace the name of Sarah Palin with, hmmm, Michelle Obama, Hillary Clinton, or Sheila Jackson Lee? How quickly would this have turned into a firestorm and all out media attack on William "Misogynist" Maher Jr.? Instead, after he made these statements William defended his actions in a later interview with ABC reporter Jake Tapper in which he claims "I'm a comedian, not just a guy who says he is..." [Tapper, March 15, 2012]. News flash, you are not a comedian. The comment wasn't funny then, it isn't funny now, and all of your directed attacks on women such as Michele Bachmann and Bristol Palin show you to be a misogynist bigot toward all conservative women. Hypocrite.

William "Misogynist" Maher Jr. has also made it very clear that he is an atheist. He has been quoted as saying:

"Religion, to me, is a bureaucracy between man and God that I don't need and let's face it; God has a big ego problem. Why do we always have to worship him?"

Note to Billy: It's not very funny, but hey, most of what you say isn't very funny. However, if that is your truth, fine. There is absolutely nothing I can say to someone like you. My response is to pray for God's mercy on you (Trust me. It ain't easy praying for you). You have made it perfectly clear that you don't believe in any religion except for the religion of government. Good for you. I hope that works out for you. My wife told me once that she would rather live her life as if there is a God even if she found out later she was wrong, than to live her life as if there is no God and discover later that there is a deity. What does she know? She is after all... crazy! Anyway, our belief in God is our choice, not yours... deal with it.

Finally, I have one more quote attributed to the television host "Misogynist" Maher:

"The tea baggers. The one thing they hate is when you call them racist. The other thing they hate is black people. But they won't say it."

Question, are you and J-Garf running in the same circles? I'm not sure what a "tea bagger" is because I don't run in your circles. Clearly you know, so tell me, what kind of tea bags do YOU like? Do you like white tea or black tea? Do these tea bags taste good? Are they flavored or unflavored? I'm just asking.

Okay, one more... let's talk about Sean Penn. A gifted actor by anyone's standard. However, he is a political imbecile. Most people have an opinion on the "gay marriage" thing and it varies depending on whom you ask. Penn said

> " ... I think that it is a good time for those who voted for the ban against gay marriage to sit and reflect and anticipate their great shame and the shame in their grandchildren's eyes if they continue that way of support. We've got to have equal rights for everyone!" [Hernandez, 2009]

Note to Sean Penn: The majority of Americans have continually reaffirmed that they do not support the concept of gay marriage. Liberal, socialist California residents even rebuked the idea when it was put to a vote.

My personal stance is that if two people of the same sex want to become a partnership such that they have the same legal standing as a married couple in the eyes of the law, I'm all for that. What I disagree with is calling it a "marriage," which is a religious covenant between a man and a woman. Call it a civil union, a couple's arrangement, or any other semantic device that appeases the Left, but it is NOT marriage as has been defined by society for centuries. The Progressives do not have the right to redefine the term. It's important to realize that only six state governments (along with the District of Columbia, the Coquille Indian Tribe, and the Suquamish tribe) have passed laws offering same-sex marriage and currently offer same-sex marriages: New York, Massachusetts, Connecticut, Iowa, Vermont, and New Hampshire. In the majority of other states, the populaces have added in their state constitutional language amendments preventing same sex marriage. The most recent of which was North Carolina in May 2012. However, don't expect this battle to subside; as always, the Progressives know what is best for us even when we tell them otherwise. It's too bad that we are not "enlightened" enough to accept their agenda, which is really just a different tactic with their war on religion.

All of the major religions of the world define marriage as a union between a man and a woman and no amount of yelling and screaming and stomping up and down by the elite Progressive teenagers is going to change that. We need to send them to their room. Let them threaten to hold their breath, just like some children threaten their parents. Eventually, they will either breathe or die, whichever comes first... it doesn't matter.

I could go on for ten more pages on the hypocrisy of the Hollywood elite. Why is it that people even pay attention to these individuals? It is not as if they have any political or real world experience. Don't get me wrong, I am not speaking about their talents as it relates to their comedic (except for Misogynist Maher) or acting abilities. Where they fall off the cliff is when they attempt to give political advice to the masses as if they possess some additional "insight" that the rest of us do not possess. Poppycock!

Actors and actresses should just leave politics out of their public comments. Hollywood is about fandom and popularity. When you speak about politics you lose both. It's a no- win situation, so my recommendation for you Hollywood-types is for you to shut up or say "no comment" when asked for your political views. It will make you appear so much smarter and I might actually still attend one of your premiere movies. If you are a "pretty face," then just be a pretty face. Are you listening, Eva Longoria? If you are a "comedian," then be a comedian and leave the political insight to the rest of us faceless morons. We can make up our own minds without your help. Trust in the people. I do.

So here is the hypocrisy. Many of these actors and actresses rail against America's policies. Here they are representing the Hollywood elite, making millions of dollars because they happen to possess a skill that puts them in the Top 1% of wage earners simply by making a single movie. Then we get buffoons like Michael "Chubby" Moore who run around with a hand-held camera to make mockumentaries, reaps in a few million dollars from the unsuspecting and uninformed youth while garnering the support of the OWS (Occupy Wall Street) crowd. I don't begrudge him making a living and reaping the rewards of his efforts. I do, however, resent the hypocrisy of his telling the rest of us to pay more taxes, to socialize our medical system, and worship the Castro way of life when he himself does none of these things he professes to support. Hypocrite.

Political and Racial Hypocrisy

Where else do we find hypocrisy in the Progressive agenda? Everywhere! Let's start with the mainstream media (MSM). An easy target is John Edwards. Of course he was the media darling during his run for the 2008 presidency. The former Democratic Senator from North Carolina was accused of using campaign funds to hide the secret of his illicit affair with reporter Rielle Hunter, while his wife at home battled cancer. As of this writing, the jury acquitted him on one count of accepting illegal campaign contributions and it deadlocked on the remaining five charges. U.S. District Judge Catherine Eagles then declared a mistrial on the remaining charges.

Here we are in the middle of an election year and if John Edwards were a Republican on trial, prior to the verdict, I'm sure it would have been the trial of the century. You and I both know that NBC, ABC, CBS, and their ilk would have been leading each evening broadcast with the details of the trial blasted on every network to ensure everyone knew he was an evil Republican - except in this case, he is a Democrat. Time will tell whether the prosecutors will seek a retrial on the remaining charges. If they do, the MSM will barely mention it if it occurs prior to the election. Mark my words.

Let's look at how race is handled by Progressives. Of course we all know what happened during the initial reporting of the Trayvon Martin case, a tragic event where the neighborhood watchman, Mark Zimmerman, who happened to be "white" Hispanic, shot a young black teenager. The immediate uproar and high-tech lynch mob created by the Left with cries of racism from the race baiters Al Sharpton, the New Black Panthers, and several Congressional representatives, went beyond the pale. This mob was prepared to have him tarred and feathered prior to any indictment or evidence being presented before a court. Spike Lee even had the audacity to tweet the guy's home address to his many followers. What did he hope to accomplish by doing that? Was he hoping that one of his followers would take matters into his or her own hands and avenge the death of Trayvon? Would Spike be complicit in a hate crime if something similar to that had occurred? Turns out Spike tweeted the wrong address and an older couple with the same last name had to move away from their home for fear of retribution. Idiot.

Here is the real hypocrisy. During the same time of the Trayvon Martin event, *The Blaze* reported the following [Gabbay, April 9, 2012]:

One city that has perennially come under fire for racially charged violence is Chicago. In just the span of three days alone — March 16th-19th of this year (2012) — 41 people, mostly African-American, were shot and killed in Chicago. Ten were killed in President Obama's former neighborhood. Incredibly, these atrocities on our very own streets barely received a turn of the head by activists, nor did they receive any media coverage.

In response to President Obama's decision to raise the profile of the Trayvon Martin case, T. Willard Fair, president of the Urban League of Greater Miami, recently told The Daily Caller *that "the outrage should be about us killing each other, about black-on-black crime."*

He asked rhetorically, "Wouldn't you think to have 41 people shot [in Chicago] between Friday morning and Monday morning would be much more newsworthy and deserve much more outrage?"

More than 500 people under the age of 21 were killed in Chicago in 2008. This figure fell only slightly in 2009 and 2010 and, of course, does not represent the many others who have been shot or injured as a result of these attacks. Records reveal that nearly 80 percent of youth homicides occurred in 22 black or Latino communities on Chicago's South and West sides.

In just the first three months of 2012, 109 people have already been murdered in the city of Chicago. So rampant are the killings in fact, that crime in the President's adopted hometown was even the focus of an April 5th report featured on The O'Reilly Factor.

Where are Jesse Jackson, Al Sharpton, Sheila Jackson Lee and the other race hustlers when these events happen in their own communities? Nowhere. Why? Because it doesn't serve the Progressive agenda.

Similarly, they don't show up when there is a clear case of black-on-white crime such as the recent incident of two reporters in Virginia. I have reprinted the article from RedState in its entirety because it points out the hypocrisy of the Left:

The "major" news media still has not seen fit to tell the story of the two white reporters attacked by a black mob in Norfolk, Virginia. Bill O'Reilly is virtually alone among major media in reporting on this, and noting that the Norfolk area "Virginia-Pilot" did not see fit to cover the local story.

Denis Finley said it was merely a "simple assault" and his paper doesn't cover such, despite the attack taking place on two of their own reporters, who were out of work from injuries for an entire week, which the police classified as "not grave injuries."

In case you missed the story, two white reporters – Dave Forster and Marjon Rostrami – had been stopped at a red light when their car was attacked by a black teen that threw a rock at the car.

When Forster got out of his stopped car to confront the rock thrower (and presumably stop further damage to his stopped car) the nearby crowd of 100 surrounded him and several started beating him violently.

When the female reporter got out of the car to try to help him she too was attacked. She managed to get a call off to police – after four attempts – and the police came to disperse the crowd.

Several things are noteworthy about this incident. I will address this in the order of what I feel is most significant, and the first, has not been addressed even on the Bill O'Reilly show.

One of the "Die Hard" movies showed what would happen to a white that is on foot in a "bad neighborhood." Our intrepid hero in that movie was forced to set out on foot in Harlem, a "bad" neighborhood – for whites. It was the major opening scene of the movie.

Did anyone complain that this depiction of what would happen to a white that is on foot in Harlem, provoke any complaints that it was exaggerated? If so I missed it.

It is a sad fact in America today that in many cities you don't want to be white and on foot in "the bad neighborhoods."

Is it because you are white and those who will attack you are black? Is it because the people there are poor and they perceive you are rich? Is it a territorial thing, i.e., you should have known better than to come into the "wrong neighborhood"?

Is this a joke? Is there anyone in America besides The Virginia Pilot's Denis Finley who says what happened to the reporter is not a hate crime, and who thinks there's nothing noteworthy about this, nothing worth their reporting on?

In fact, if this is not noteworthy, if this is not worthy of a news story in the Norfolk newspaper or in any national media (except for The Blaze online and Bill O'Reilly on Fox TV) then it proves my first point.

Of course, there's nothing unusual about this story because everybody knows if you are white and you get out of your car in an inner city, high crime, black neighborhood, you will do well to escape with your life, and you will very likely be beaten and robbed very shortly.

It is nice to see that the police, after a few weeks of news silence on this story, did finally arrest a 16 year old for this crime – and he is now an accused felon.

And, since the outcry generated from Bill O'Reilly's Fox news report, the editor has at least attempted to make excuses. Finley wrote that he had (at last) discovered that "race has entered the equation." You think?

And, the solicitous Finley also wrote that he'd not reported on the story earlier because his two suddenly bashful reporters did not want their names in the news. One wonders if he is usually this solicitous with other crime victims.

My further conclusions from this story, aside from the fact that everybody KNOWS it is dangerous to be white and on foot in an inner city in America, and everybody knows you aren't supposed to say or write this, follows.

First, and most fundamental, is that it is only marginally LESS safe to be a black stranger, dressed upscale, and appearing to NOT BELONG to that neighborhood, and be on foot in a black neighborhood. Black on black crime, like the Rodney King riots of many years ago, is the under reported news in America's inner cities.

The biggest victims of black criminals are blacks who live in their inner city territory. Not the rare white who happens to have made the mistake of being on foot, or stopped at a traffic light, in such a "territory."

Second. Bill O'Reilly makes the point that Denis Finley denies: if this were a story in Norfolk, Virginia (or any other city in America) of a gang of whites attacking a nice, young couple who happened to have been stopped at a traffic light, we'd have been seeing 24/7 news coverage of this on all the network news channels, radio stations and newspapers in America, for the last few weeks.

Far LESS of a racial motivation has been shown in the Trayvon Martin case in Florida, but the intensity of the media coverage has been incredible.

Third. There is an undertone to this story, if you read between the lines, that the white couple were stupid to have driven their car in that neighborhood, deserved what happened to them. And that they were extra stupid to have got out of their car.

This "blame the victim" mentality of course, completely excuses the criminal. Of course it is true – if they hadn't been in that neighborhood, and just drove off (including RUN THE RED LIGHT, ESCAPE!!!!), they would not have been hurt. But this "blame the victim" thing is pretty awful, in my view.

Fourth. The liberal media operates on a double standard. Of course they are not going to cover a story like this. Liberals HATE stories like this because they think it plays into the hands of conservatives who are all male racists (according to them).

A story like this would seem to justify their bad behavior so it should not be covered at all.

Fifth. There is a paternalistic mentality at work here on the part of the liberal media. They think you should not hold black criminals to the same standards as criminal whites. They will excuse behavior of blacks, which they would never excuse for whites, because they actually think blacks are stupid, inferior.

They are pathetically racist with this mentality.

Sixth. Many who read this may be shocked but, there is actually a mentality among the liberal-left that says the crimes of whites against blacks – starting with the crime of slavery – is the reason that blacks have a lesser standard of living in the United States, and that only reparations paid by whites to compensate for the several generations of "criminal conduct" against them, will balance this equation.

This is not the mentality of socialist "spread the wealth around" which we have seen and heard from Barack Obama and other leftists. This is reparation for "crimes" by whites against blacks.

Of course this is silly.

Why would a black who came here from Jamaica or from Nigeria three years ago, need "reparations" to pay for what happened to a black slave over 100 years ago?

Why would an Asian Indian or a Russian who drives a taxi in New York City since they arrived in America five years ago, be required to "pay" for the supposed crimes of whites over 100 years ago?

Why would the descendants of people who "gave the last full measure of devotion" on the battlefield to end slavery, as commemorated in

Lincoln's Gettysburg Address, be required to pay reparations?

Why would the side that won a victory at Gettysburg for the idea that you do not have to pay for the crimes of your parents nor have a title or other "tradition" bestowed on you based upon the accident of your birth, now be told that they must pay "reparations" for the supposed sins of their great grandparents?

How did we get to this point in America where an attack like this is covered up instead of reported for what it is – an indication that there is a problem with the criminal justice system in America, especially in our cities, and that there are too many underage inner city troublemakers roaming about without jobs, without hope, but with plenty of bitterness and rage?

How did we get to the point in America that in most cities everybody seems to think a crime like this is not a wakeup call for us to take action but a sign that two white people were in the wrong place and at the wrong time?

Seventh. The argument was actually offered on camera by someone from the neighborhood to Bill O'Reilly's producer that the attack by a black mob on two whites was to get even for the death of black Trayvon Martin in Florida.

This is ridiculous on several levels. First, two wrongs don't make a right. Second, the facts of the two cases *are totally different and in Florida are in dispute but there is no disputing that the two white reporters did not attack the black gang. Third, and most important: there were loud and repeated demands that the white be arrested during 24/7 news coverage of the Trayvon Martin case. There has been a media blackout of the Norfolk, Virginia incident.*

Eighth. Finally, irony about the story. The girl is from Iran. If a group of whites had attacked her, would that have generated a media firestorm? Would we have seen an outpouring of "Muslim immigrant attacked by American mob" or "Female Iranian Immigrant assaulted by The Ugly Americans" for 24/7? Would we have seen repeated demands that the criminals who assaulted her should be found and arrested?

What happened to Dave Forster and Marjon Rostrami is wrong. Skin color should not enter into this topic except to note that it was clearly a motivation on the part of their attackers.

It is wrong, and we should be asking the question about American cities which Dr. Edward Banfield wrote about in The Unheavenly City (1970) – liberal solutions add to the decay, boost the frustration and bitterness, skyrocket the crime rate and solve nothing.

Banfield was not any kind of a "movement conservative" but if you accept the premise that sometimes, we ought to look at issues from a "right and wrong" perspective, then he offers a lot of reasons why liberalism in American cities doesn't ever work, and why conservative ideas (such as the enterprise zones his book helped motivate/inspire) should be tried instead.

If you keep boosting taxes in American cities and driving off business and the middle class you end up with an ever increasing number of gangs roaming about, looking for some hapless person to stop at a red light where they can throw a rock or do worse.

Liberals have had virtual monopoly control of most of America's cities for several generations and the ugly truth is, their ideas don't work, but make it worse, to the point it is now very dangerous in the cities they control. It isn't hard to see why there is so much "flight" to the suburbs from the cities of America.

The question isn't what happened in Norfolk on May 1 to two white reporters. Nor is it, what motivated a gang of troublemakers, nor even why is it liberal media covers up stories like this?

Rather, the question is, what is happening to America's cities, and what can we do to reverse the trend that makes it dangerous to stop at a red light in the wrong neighborhood in so many cities in America?

Note: The above article came from *Hanover Henry of RED STATE who is Pat Henry on Facebook. You can communicate to him directly via private mail at Facebook.

I have come to the conclusion that racism is no longer taken as a serious issue in this country. Serious in the sense of doing anything about it. Cries of "racism" from Democrats are now merely a tactic. The Left uses it as a sword in an attempt to silence others when they don't agree with the policies of Barack Obama. It is used to vilify groups who don't agree with the policies of the Left. It is used to target and smear individuals who don't bow to the Progressive agenda. It is used and used and used and I, like many others, have grown weary. The racism sword is no longer sharp, it is merely a blunt instrument being swung in every direction to bludgeon anyone in its path.

When the New Black Panthers threatened voters at a poll site in Philadelphia during the 2008 election, where was the condemnation from the race hustlers during this episode of voter intimidation? If this had been the KKK at a poll site in Alabama doing the exact same thing, well we know what the response would be, and we know how it would be covered by the MSM. Progressives are hypocrites.

When the Democrats who have controlled the cities of Oakland, Detroit, Chicago, etc. actually start doing something to eliminate minority dependency on government entitlements and put in policies that create real wealth, create real jobs in their neighborhoods, and provide people an opportunity to get ahead in society, then and only then should we talk about racism. It is time to get minorities off the plantation.

I recently came across an article that shows the failure of the policies of Progressives. If this doesn't open the eyes of independent voters and more Democrats, then may God be with them in their march to hell.

There is an interesting fact regarding America's poorest cities, all large population centers, spread across wide regions of the U.S. Most have had Democrat or Progressive mayors and councils for many decades. A few have not elected a Republican mayor or council throughout the 20th century and not yet in the 21st century. Most have had Democrats in control for 50 years or more.

Liberals constantly bombard us with the need for their agenda and policies to be implemented to help the disadvantaged. Many of the country's disadvantaged live in large numbers in the cities noted and Democrats and liberals have had full fetter to implement their ideas, policies and agendas for a long, long time. Yet the cities do not seem to improve.

We're told more money, more entitlements and more liberal policies must be allowed in these cities and, due to the long Democrat control, this continues to be done. The cities, though, now tell us they must lay off workers, fire fighters, police officers, close libraries, municipal swimming pools, cut other essential services. Regardless, the Democrats maintain they must be re-elected so that they can implement more policies and entitlements and taxes to get the job done.

Some stats from the US Census Bureau in an American Community survey, August 2007:

The top 13 cities with the most people below the poverty level, (population 500,000+)

1. Bronx, NY (housing, pop. 1,332,650): 30.7%

2. Detroit, MI (housing, pop. 871,121): 26.1%

    Detroit hasn't elected a Republican mayor since 1961

3. Brooklyn, NY (housing, pop. 2,465,326): 25.1%

4. Baltimore, MD (housing, pop. 631,366): 22.9%

    Baltimore hasn't elected a Republican since 1963

5. Philadelphia, PA (housing, pop. 1,448,394): 22.9%

    Philadelphia hasn't elected a Republican mayor since 1952

6. El Paso, TX (housing, pop. 609,415): 22.2%

    El Paso has never had a Republican mayor

7. Los Angeles, CA (housing, pop. 3,849,378): 22.1%

Los Angeles hasn't had a Republican mayor since 2001

8. Milwaukee, WI (housing, pop. 573,358): 21.4%

    Milwaukee hasn't elected a Republican mayor since 1906

9. New York, NY (housing, pop. 8,214,426): 21.3%

10. Manhattan, NY (housing, pop. 1,537,195): 20.0%

11. Chicago, IL (housing, pop. 2,833,321): 19.6%

    Chicago hasn't elected a Republican mayor since 1927

12. Boston, MA (housing, pop. 590,763): 19.5%

    Boston hasn't elected a Republican mayor since 1926

13. Houston, TX (housing, pop. 2,144,491): 19.2%

    Houston elected its last Republican mayor in 1978

Note: the boroughs of New York (the Bronx, Brooklyn, Manhattan, and New York City) all are in the top percent of poverty towns. As of this writing, the current mayor of New York City is "Nanny" Michael Bloomberg, who ran as a Republican in 2002 and who reclassified himself as an Independent in 2007. Despite his label, Bloomberg is a Progressive statist.

It makes you wonder, based on this history of performance, what's going on? I believe it was Einstein who stated that "The definition of insanity is doing the same thing over and over again and expecting different results." Why do these cities keep putting the same people and party back in power? Simple, it is not about helping people OUT of poverty, it is about keeping people IN poverty and dependent in order for the Democratic Party to remain IN power. The Democrats have clearly succeeded in these major cities to be the only voices heard by the masses. The liberal Progressive plantation owners keep promising the slaves that they will make their life better, easier, and that they will take care of them. Unfortunately, the minority and poverty stricken communities still listen to and believe in their slave masters. It's sad.

So here is my proposed response to their tactics. Since cries of racism are only a tactic, conservatives should ignore any and all future claims of racism or hate crimes "from the Left." That's right, ignore them completely, just like they ignore black-on-white or black-on-black crime. Whenever they scream "Racist!" conservatives should repeat what they say in Texas, "That dog don't hunt."

I'm not saying racism doesn't still exist in America (as a black man, I have experienced first-hand incidences and inconveniences of racist behavior), but the Democrats and Progressives now use it as a tool to keep minorities in their pocket and to silence conservatives. Notice how the Democrats use racism during every election cycle to rally their base and fall silent immediately after the election. They don't care. They are hypocrites. Ignore their claims. Listen up. When your teenager screams and shouts, what should you as a responsible parent do? Ignore the teenager and send him to his room. You will discover their bark is harmless. The race baiters have cried "wolf" once too many times. Remember, it is a tactic to get what they want. IGNORE the screaming baby in the room, eventually, it will go to sleep. Let it cry itself to sleep.

Green Energy is a Black Hole

So is ANYONE paying attention to the Obama Administration's war on the energy industry, especially energy producers and energy consumers? Prior to taking office, former Senator Obama was very clear in his intent to impose a Cap and Trade policy on the energy industry. In January 2008, he stated that

> "Under my plan of a cap and trade system, electricity price would necessarily skyrocket. . . . Because I'm capping greenhouse gases, coal power plants, natural gas—you name it—whatever the plants were, whatever the industry was, they would have to retrofit their operations. That will cost money. They will pass that money on to consumers."

He followed up his comment with

> "So if somebody wants to build a coal-powered plant, they can. It's just that it will bankrupt them,

*because they're going to be charged a huge sum
for all that greenhouse gas that's being emitted."*

So President Barack Obama's energy agenda is tied to the Progressive wing's global warming agenda (thank you, Al Gore). The global warming agenda is nothing more than a faux-scientific rationale for wealth redistribution. The wealth redistribution was to occur through a cap and trade system where the more industrious energy-hogging countries (such as the United States and China) would purchase carbon credits (CO2 permits) from the less advanced energy countries (places like Zimbabwe and other third world countries, which have nothing else to sell).

I know I will be called a "flat-earther" for denying the existence of global warming. Fine. I've never denied that the earth may be warming, nor have I denied that the earth may be cooling. What I am questioning is the assumed relationship between man-made carbon dioxide (CO2) in the atmosphere and the purported changes in global temperatures proclaimed by the alarmists! I am not going to turn this into a scientific treatise, because as I have said before, facts mean nothing to Liberals... it's all about the Progressive agenda for them. I will ask one question that all the Intergovernmental Panel on Climate Change (IPCC) scientists always seem to ignore, i.e., "What is the largest greenhouse gas in our atmosphere?" Anyone care to guess? The answer is water vapor... by a large margin! Guess what happens with too much water vapor. You get clouds. We all know what happens with too many clouds in the sky. You get rain! What does rain do? It gets us wet. Scary stuff.

Note to the environmental climate Nazis: water vapor contributes anywhere between 36%-72% to greenhouse gas effects, whereas carbon dioxide only contributes between 9%-26% at most! So why are we wanting to put all of our efforts on limiting CO2 emissions, when obviously the real culprit is water vapor? The answer is easy. Since 70% of the earth's surface is covered by water, even the radical environmental loonies knew they couldn't put limits on water use and get the population to buy in. I can hear it now when an EPA regulator shows up at my doorstep for using water, because it contributes to global warming. My response to this bureaucrat will be:

"You want to charge me HOW MUCH for watering my [lawn, garden, farm, etc.]? Are you fricking kidding me? Screw the planet and screw you! I'm watering and I'm not paying you a damn nickel more to save the planet! Get the hell away from me and stay away from my wallet!"

So these redistributionists decided to pick a more "plausible" foe. Carbon dioxide became the enemy, and fossil fuels became the culprit. In order to save the planet and the world's environment, we need to reduce our dependence on fossil fuel. Don't get caught up in the global warming poppycock! As J-Garf would say, "This is nothing more than straight-up world socialism! The one-world globalists want to take wealth away from the energy- producing rich countries and reallocate to the poorer nations."

This is how it would work. Some central body known as the carbon credit exchange would distribute carbon credit permits. These credits would be created out of thin air and allocated around the world. Countries, states, industries, and companies would be able to use these allocated carbon credits as they used energy. So, now each country, state, industry, or company has a choice. They can either improve their energy efficiency with major capital investments to stay within their allocated amount of credits, or they can purchase additional carbon credits from a country that isn't using all of its allocation because it lacks an energy industry and, hence, won't need all of its allocated credits. Either way, the consumer gets screwed because he or she will have to pay for these additional credits or capital investments through higher fees and energy costs. Who will this impact the most? The poorest communities on fixed incomes. I told you that Progressives are hypocrites! They really don't care about the poor and downtrodden.

Here is the kicker. The carbon credit exchange would put Caps (limits) on how many credits any particular country, state, industry, or company could receive. Anyone wanting additional credits would be required to purchase these through the exchange from those poorer nations, who would trade credits for money. The perfect wealth redistribution scheme. Nice, huh?

Progressives think we are stupid. We are not. The primary reason I did not and could not vote for Obama was because of his energy policy. I knew then that his war on fossil fuels would have a devastating impact on this country. I also understood that when the President talks about redistribution of wealth (as he did with Joe the plumber), his sights are not focused within the United States.

President Obama intends to redistribute wealth from the United States to the rest of the undeveloped world and, in so doing, the net effect will be lowering our standard of living.

Why else would Barack Obama agree to pay $2 billion dollars to help Brazil perform deep-water drilling off their coast while limiting the amount of drilling permits in our own coastal waters? Why? Is he an idiot? No, he is what he says he is... a wealth redistributionist. Note to all of my black folks out there who thought you were going to receive your Obama checks. You better pack up and move to a third world country outside the United States if you expect to receive more Obama money. Black folks need to get with the program and see the big picture. Barack is NOT the "One" and he has no intention of saving you. He wants to be your slave master and unfortunately many of you behave like some of the freed slaves did after the Civil War, they didn't want to leave the plantation. Don't be one of those slaves.

Finally, we can't talk about energy and ignore how this administration has used the Department of Energy as a funnel to shuffle money – taxpayer money – to its political allies and supporters. Now you understand the "green agenda" is nothing more than a socialist ploy to redistribute wealth (your wealth) to foreign countries. How has the Obama administration been using the "green agenda?" According to research done by Hoover Institution Fellow Peter Schweizer in his book *Throw Them All Out,* the hundreds of millions of dollars in taxpayer-backed loans handed to Solyndra – the now bankrupt solar company that was run by Obama campaign bundler George Kaiser – is just the "tip of the iceberg."

In fact, a staggering 80% of the federal grants and loan guarantees made to green-tech firms by Obama's DOE since 2009 were "made to companies whose chief executive or chief investors were major contributors and big money men to Obama's 2008 presidential campaign." This should be a red flag to every tax-paying citizen in the United States. President Obama and his Administration are using our taxpayer funds to reward his supporters. As J-Garf would say, "This is nothing but straight up crony capitalism!" The numbers we are talking about are staggering. According to a recent House Oversight Committee Report, the DOE's 1705 green loan program had approved 27 project loans totaling more than $14.5 billion. Recall how long it takes to hand out a billion dollars. If you are an Obama campaign bundler of donations, you too can receive hundreds of millions of dollars in loan guarantees. Coincidence? What do you think?

Maybe it wouldn't be so bad if at least a few of these company investments had panned out and actually created a few American jobs. Instead we have Solyndra, First Solar, Brightsource, NRG Energy, SolarReserve, and even Fisker Automotive who was given $529 million taxpayer dollars to assemble electric cars in Finland. Finland? Yes, as I claimed earlier, the green agenda is a ruse to redistribute wealth. Except this time the redistribution is going to wealthy CEO's who are friends of Obama. They give him campaign money; he gives them your taxpayer dollars. Everybody wins, except "we the people." How much longer can we put up with this? Remember how the Left use to scream about the Bush-Cheney relationship with Halliburton and all of the crony capitalism in the Bush Administration. Where are those critics now? What are we hearing from the Left? Crickets. President Obama and his Progressive crowd are hypocrites.

Bottom line: the richest countries in the world with the highest standard of living for their people are countries that use and produce energy. Energy is the lifeblood of a thriving modern society. All forms of energy should be harnessed (especially fossil fuels) based on the needs of and economic impact on the local community. President Obama won't approve the Keystone Pipeline that would transfer tar oil from the sands in northeastern Canada down to Texas to be refined and distributed. Why? This has nothing to do with environmental safety reasons. There are many Progressive and environmental extremists who believe we as a nation use too much of the world's energy resources. Therefore, the United States should reduce its energy needs, period. What those same people fail to realize is if you take away energy, then the society that depends upon it will quickly decay. Is that the ultimate goal of the Progressive agenda? Are there actually people in this country who want to take down the cultural, political, and economic system we call the United States? We see the Obama regime behaving as Ronald Reagan said all progressive regimes behave toward business:

> "If it moves, tax it. If it keeps moving, regulate it. And if it stops moving, subsidize it."

That appears to be the Obama agenda on energy. Fossil fuels are being taxed. Carbon emissions are being heavily regulated. And "green energy," which can't survive in the free market, is being subsidized by taxpayer dollars.

There is absolutely no reason for this country not to be energy independent. We have both the technical prowess and the natural resources to enable independence within a relatively short period of time (10 years or less). We only need the political leadership and the release of the entrepreneurial "can-do" American spirit to become the world's largest energy producer. It's time for the people to tell their politicians to start thinking about America first on energy policy. We shouldn't have to buy a single barrel of oil from any tin-pot dictator, sheikh, or political head that leads a country that despises America. There is no reason to continually finance regimes that don't have our best interests at heart. Developing our energy resources brings the best promise of true economic development for this nation. This issue, more than anything else, is why I did not vote for Obama in 2008 or 2012.

The Abortion Thing

The Progressives have imposed the biggest hate crime on black Americans when we talk about the evils of Planned Parenthood. Think about that term "hate crime" for a second. What the heck does that mean? A crime is a crime, and it doesn't matter who the perpetrator is or who the victims are. If a law is broken and someone's individual rights are violated, the perpetrator should be prosecuted to the full extent of the law. Period.

However, in the case of abortions, I may show my own hypocrisy by classifying abortion as a "hate crime." Remember, until 2008 I was a classic liberal and I believed in pro-choice. It all sounded right to me and fundamentally it seemed like it was up to the woman as to whether to bring a pregnancy to term.

However, what I didn't know, even though it is a well-documented fact (although not very well promoted by Liberals) was that Margaret Sanger who believed in eugenics created Planned Parenthood. Just like Hitler tried to exterminate the Jews, Margaret Sanger wanted to prevent Blacks from breeding because she felt they were a drain on society. Michelle Malkin wrote an excellent piece "To Stop the Multiplication of the Unfit" in February of 2012, where she pointed out that Margaret Sanger

> "...founded Planned Parenthood in 1916 'to stop the multiplication of the unfit.' This, she boasted, would be 'the most important and greatest step towards race betterment.' While she oversaw the mass murder of black babies, Sanger cynically recruited minority activists to front her death racket. She conspired with eugenics financier and businessman Clarence Gamble to 'hire three or four colored ministers, preferably with social-service backgrounds, and with engaging personalities' to sell their genocidal policies as community health

and welfare services... Sanger and Gamble called their deadly campaign The Negro Project."

Those of you out there promoting a woman's right to choose - ask yourself, who are you killing? Planned Parenthood sounds almost Orwellian when used in this context. It is the exact opposite. It is Planned Un-Parenthood. It is the murder of children, which was specifically designed with the intent of genocide against the minority community. Did you know that? I certainly did not.

I'm a Christian and I have faith in God. As an engineer, I had to step back and ask myself a logical pragmatic question on the issue of abortion: "When does life begin?" The only logical conclusion isn't when the fetus is viable, or the 2nd trimester, or at birth. Anyone who thinks about the subject for more than a minute must conclude that life begins at conception. Period. Hence on matters of abortion, a woman's right to choose occurs when she decides to have unprotected sex with a man. After conception occurs, there is a new separate life on our hands and according to our own Deck-of-I:

"We hold these truths to be self-evident, that all men are created equal, that they are endowed by their Creator with certain unalienable Rights, that among these are Life, Liberty and the Pursuit of Happiness: –That to secure these rights, Governments are instituted among Men, deriving their just powers from the Consent of the governed..."

If we are to follow our Deck-of-I and the Constitution, it is the responsibility of Government to secure our unalienable Rights. Yes, I understand there are instances of rape and incest, but what percentage of pregnancies are a result of rape or incest? Anyone know? This is a hard choice for me, as I'm sure it is for anyone put in this situation. In the case of rape and incest, the choice is a deeply personal one between the woman, her physician, and God. Whether she decides to carry the baby to term and offer him or her up for adoption, or to terminate the pregnancy is a choice only she can make.

I will end this chapter on hypocrisy by using a variation of the words attributed to Sean Penn earlier:

> *"I think that it is a good time for those who support abortion to sit and reflect and anticipate their great shame and the shame in their grandchildren's eyes if they continue that way of support. We've got to have equal rights for everyone, even the unborn!"*

Do social issues matter? Yes, but not as much as fundamental principles. The difference between the left and the right is that each starts from a very different fundamental value system. If your principles define you, then all of your decisions will be based on those principles. This is a good time to reflect on the value system of the Liberal left. Forget the stupid arguments about "rights"... we were all born with the same rights. By focusing on principles, the Progressive, Liberal, Socialist Left collapses... they have none.

Chapter 5

Politics are Personal

1. A diary is forever.

2. Liberal friends and family. Love them, but just know they won't change.

3. Liberals excel on not agreeing on the facts.

4. Scott Walker makes history!

Grasshopper's Diary:

Saturday, January 2, 2010

Well, my goal is to write at least 10 minutes a day to document what I believe is going on in our country, and in my life. Last year was interesting, as Ant and I learned about the devaluation of the dollar, investing in gold and the creeping advancement of socialism in our government. Even though we did not vote for Obama, we were both excited by the thought we had our first black president. However, it did not take long to realize that this President leaned way too far to the radical Left. I believe President Obama could have been the greatest president EVER if he had governed FROM the center. Unfortunately, he is an ideologue. Spending our country into an all-time debt crisis; wanting to put Muslim jihadist terrorists on trial in NYC and close down Guantanamo Bay; and get this, now Eric Holder from the Justice Department wants to move all the detainees to a prison in Illinois! Will somebody tell me the difference between holding them in Cuba or holding them in Illinois? Nothing makes sense anymore. There was a shooting at Fort Hood. The accused is Muslim. We had what is called "the Underwear Bomber," who attempted to blow up a plane from Amsterdam to Detroit. The arrested culprit was Muslim. The day after Christmas when I landed in Albuquerque, a reporter interviewed me and asked how I felt about safety for the flying public? I wish I had said that we need to profile people boarding the plane, but I didn't. I didn't want the word "racist" associated with my name if they decided to air it on the news. What a wimp I was... next time.

Stories from the Front Line

In the course of writing this book, I have spent countless number of hours in front of my computer typing and editing. Based on the early readings from Grasshopper, it appears to me that every 3-4 hours of my personal time, amounts to approximately 10 minutes of reading material in this book. I am an incredibly slow writer. It's pitiful. My problem is I think too much. I evaluate and continually self-edit, and only then do I write something down on paper. I hate it. I envy people who can easily write. I also have an appreciation for those who have the steadfastness to stay with it. For me, it's been quite an investment of time to put something in print that may interest no one but my wife and me. However, I am on a mission to get this done and while I have no clue how to publish and distribute a book such as this, somehow, someway, I am confident it will happen as soon as I complete it. How do I know? Faith.

So the other day while at work, I had a bit of a scare. I was in a meeting with my boss and as I was writing stuff in my engineering notebook, all of a sudden my hand stopped responding to my brain and I couldn't write. I had a tingling sensation down my right arm from the elbow down, but my hand wasn't responding. I put the pen down and didn't take notes the rest of the meeting. I forgot about it afterwards and went home that night without a second thought (typical guy behavior). On the following day, the same thing happened in my office around 2 pm when I was transcribing some notes and again, all of a sudden, I couldn't write... I was staring at the pen in my hand and even with effort, it would not move. So I went outside my office and asked my assistant Debra and my business manager Tracy who happened to be standing outside my office if they had experienced anything like this. Tracy looked at me and exclaimed, "You need to go to the Doctor NOW. You may be having a stroke." I said, "It doesn't feel like a stroke." Not that I know what one feels like, but I wasn't light-headed, dizzy, or anything one might associate with a stroke. My speech wasn't slurred, I just couldn't write.

So, a colleague, Edward, agreed to walk over to the onsite medical clinic with me to make sure I made it. Tracy insisted that Edward go along as she was convinced I would collapse in an epileptic seizure on the sidewalk en-route. I checked in and after a few minutes in the waiting room, my name was called and a nurse took my blood pressure... 130 over 73, not bad. My temperature was 98.4. Again, nothing suspicious here.

Finally, a doctor's aid came in and performed a few tests on me. He made me touch all of my fingers with my thumb, he tested for strength, dexterity, etc. He asked again if I hurt anywhere while he worked his way to my funny bone and applied pressure. It sent a lightning shock wave up and down my arm… I nearly jumped out of my seat when he touched it. Then he asked the perfect question: "Have you done any physical cranking with your arm over the weekend?" I thought for a second, and realized that my wife had bought a set of outdoor furniture that I helped to assemble the previous weekend. I was using a wrench to put that monstrosity together and apparently, I had inflamed my ulnar nerve from too much torque. The ulnar nerve runs from the shoulder, through the funny bone to the hand and is responsible for carrying signals between the hand and the brain. What I didn't realize at the time was that an injury to the ulnar nerve can damage the communication path to your hand and thus limit motion and feeling in the hand and forearm. That was it! It explained the symptoms, my lack of pain elsewhere, and the fact that I could still smile and I wasn't turning into a blithering village idiot. Thank god it wasn't a stroke! Right? The moral of the story… no more honey-do's for my crazy wife!

I thought it might be instructive to hear some of my wife's thoughts as she kept a diary for most of 2010. You can decide if you think she is crazy or not.

Grasshopper's Diary: Sunday, January 3, 2010

Beautiful day. Not a cloud in the sky. The kind of sky that is so blue against the mountains. I watched Fox Sunday. The talk was of the Administration's failure on the Flight 283 mishap. The Administration plans to put Umar Farouk Abdulmutallab, a.k.a. the "Underwear Bomber" on trial as a civilian. WTF! I think this is crazy. He is not a civilian. He is an enemy combatant.

I am getting so tired of our government's politically correct lawyers. Is this their way to make others like us? How idiotic is that? Our government is out of whack. Then, on the ABC news show, some lady from the Atlantic Constitution Journal was talking about how they had to give a little bit of pork to Senator Nelson to be able to pass the healthcare bill. Who is drinking this Kool-Aid? Why do the other states have to pay for the Medicare and/or Medicaid of Nebraska residents? A Cornhusker Kickback of hundreds of billions of dollars... yeah, I would say that's a little bit of pork. What happened to "no pork" Obama?

Grasshopper's Diary: Tuesday, January 5, 2010

I think I am going to keep a "Reasons I Like Sarah Palin" file. This was the latest on what she wrote on her Facebook:

"President Obama's meeting with his top national security advisors does nothing to change the fact that his fundamental approach to terrorism is fatally flawed. We are at war with radical Islamic extremists and treating this threat as a law enforcement issue is dangerous for our nation's security. That's what happened in the 1990s and we saw the result on September 11, 2001. This is a war on terror not an "overseas contingency operation." Acts of terrorism are just that, not "man caused disasters." The system did not work. Abdulmutallab was a child of privilege radicalized and trained by organized jihadists, not an "isolated extremist" who traveled to a land of "crushing poverty." He is an enemy of the United States, not just another criminal defendant."

What's interesting to me is that the people who really hate Sarah Palin say it's not because of her policies, but because they think she is stupid. I ask all the time for her critics to give me an example of her so called "stupidity." Still waiting. Most people will just believe what the lame steam media spews out to them. Having a policy disagreement with a person is different than saying the person is stupid. I don't agree with Obama, but I don't call him stupid. I think his actions are stupid, but that is a policy disagreement I have with him.

Grasshopper's Diary: January 7, 2010

Well, I skipped yesterday. It took only six days to fail my New Year's resolution for 2010. Oh well. While I was in the shower this morning, I was thinking about when Hurricane Katrina hit New Orleans and wondered why those poor people sat around waiting for the government to take care of them instead of trying to take care of themselves. What if the people on Flight 283 had waited for someone on their flight to take care of the "underwear bomber" instead of acting on their own? They would all be dead. What if the people in Iowa just sat in their homes waiting for the government to take care of them when the floodwaters rose in 2009, instead of building dikes, and taking care of themselves? Welfare begets dependency and if anyone truly thinks a government gives a damn about you as an individual, you are dead wrong. You are just a vote to them, a name on a piece of paper. People need to learn to be responsible for themselves, whether in good times or bad times. God gave us a brain and free will. We should take advantage of both to look out for our family and ourselves.

Grasshopper's Diary: January 9, 2010

Ant is reading a book called *"The 5000 Year Leap."* The premise is that our Founding Fathers understood freedom and individual rights. The author, W. Cleon Skousen, wrote about the Founding Fathers in his dedication:

> *"They created a new cultural climate that gave wings to the human spirit. They encouraged exploration to reveal the scientific secrets of the universe. They built a free-enterprise culture to encourage industry and prosperity. They gave humanity the needed ingredients for a gigantic 5,000-year leap!"*

Ant read to me from the book this morning and it is obvious that we have moved so far from what our Founding Fathers intended for this nation. The concept of wealth redistribution and the "Robin Hood" mentality of stealing from the rich to give to the poor will forever damage this country, if we don't stop it now. Ant read a section of the book that made sense to me. Apparently, there was a time in Russia when the government came in and stole from the wealthy farmers and gave the land to the peasants. The peasants all cheered this move by the government. Later, the government returned and took the land from the peasants for government use. There was no cheering. This is the path we are on. I don't understand why this isn't obvious to the American people. This so called Utopia they seek has never worked. I would rather we all be unequally wealthy, whether by hard work, good luck, or serendipity, than be equally poor. If we are equally poor, than no one is available to lift up those who need lifting... except for the government, which put us in that position.

In *The 5000 Year Leap*, Skousen wrote:

"President Grover Cleveland vetoed legislation in his day designed to spend federal taxes for private welfare problems. He wrote:

'I can find no warrant for such an appropriation in the Constitution, and I do not believe that the power and duty of the General Government ought to be extended to the relief of individual suffering which is in no manner properly related to the public service or benefit. A prevalent tendency to disregard the limited mission of this power and duty should, I think, be steadfastly resisted, to the end that the lesson should be constantly enforced that though the people support the Government the Government should not support the people...

The friendliness and charity of our countrymen can always be relied upon to relieve their fellow-citizens in misfortune.' "

Look how far removed we are from that mindset today. Don't count on the government. Those of you who believe President Obama is different, I urge you to watch what he does, not what he says.

Grasshopper's Diary: January 15, 2010

I know, I know, it's been six more days. This is harder than I thought. The Democratic Party is really the Party of racists and has fooled people for too many years. I guess when Bill Clinton stated that "...Barack would have been pouring my coffee a few years ago..." that was not considered a racist comment. I guess when Senator Harry Reid referred to Senator Barack Obama as "light skinned and no Negro dialect," I suppose that was not a racist comment. I guess when Joe Biden says that "Barack is clean cut and well spoken," that should not be construed as a racist comment. Good Lord, listen to those comments. Who says stuff like that?? Liberal Democrats.

Ant and I were in a restaurant in Fort Worth and I came across a friend and introduced Ant to the friend and her mother. Later, I walked by their table and the mother said to me that Ant is so nice looking and so well spoken. I knew she meant it as a compliment, but would she have said that if Ant were white? Would Biden have said that about Barack if he were ALL white? Think about that. Blacks have bought into the Democratic Party line for the last 50 years and all they have to show for it is more welfare, fractured families, poor education, and the abortion of many, many black babies. When will they wake up? Show me a city that is under a Progressive regime that is prospering... Detroit? If the black community was diverse in its political affiliations and election of officials, then the Democratic Party could not own you and they would have to do right by you. Right now, the Democratic Party keeps feeding the black community B.S. about how the Republican Party wants to take away your entitlements. Black communities everywhere are still in shambles. The Democratic Party owns you and you are not holding them accountable.

Slavery was wrong then and it is now. I pray for the day the black community will wake up.

After writing this, I came across the following in an OpEd (source unknown) today:

> As Martin Luther King Jr. once put it, "I have a dream that my four little children will one day live in a nation where they will not be judged by the color of their skin but by the content of their character." Democrats still have that reversed: "I have a dream that my children will one day live in a nation where they will not be judged by the content of their character but by the color of their skin." What's truly racist is that Democrats demand absolute allegiance and ideological purity from blacks, in effect keeping their prized constituency on the modern-day plantation."

Grasshopper's Diary: January 19, 2010

Ant flew to DC yesterday. Today is the special election for the replacement of Ted Kennedy's vacancy in the US Senate seat in MA. Scott Brown, the Republican candidate actually has a shot. In fact, he is ahead in all polls. This is truly amazing. If this happens, maybe we can stop this madness of health care reform. Now mind you, I'm all for healthcare reform, just not this healthcare reform which isn't reform at all. For the Progressives, this is all about control. If it truly were about healthcare, then we would also have tort reform, free market insurance competition across state lines, and we would not have abortion-on-demand being funded by our federal dollars.

Granted, I am pro-life and yet I understand that abortion is legal. But by God, I don't believe MY federal tax dollars should be spent on abortion. Choice, right? That's not my choice. I'll get back to you after the election results tonight. These are very exciting times.

Grasshopper's Diary: January 20, 2010

Great Scott! Good Lord, I can't believe it. A fiscal conservative won a Senate seat in Massachusetts, the bluest of all states! People, this was about policy. Fundamentally, we are a center-right country, and when politicians start telling us what they think is best for us, it's time to tell Washington that the power resides with the people. Thank you, Massachusetts.

Last night I couldn't sleep because of the election, and I started thinking about Saul Alinsky's "Rules for Radicals" far left tactics to hijack this country. Alinsky had a plan, but during the time when he drew up the plan, he did not know there would be an Internet, or conservative talk radio, or Fox News. He thought he could spoon-feed his ideology to the useful idiots and that they would help bring down the United States of America. The American people are not stupid and the majority of us do not want to tear down the best system on earth. The TEA Party movement is not a bunch of white, uneducated rednecks. In fact, we are a very politically diverse community from all different walks of life. The Liberal Left thinks if you say something enough, it will become a fact. I'm repeatedly hearing in the MSM how stupid, ignorant, racist, [pick your negative adjective] the people are in the TEA Party movement. We are pushing back. Truth will always win out, always. We are not stupid. In fact, this movement is well informed. That is why members of Congress, such as Nancy Pelosi, vilify the TEA Party. We are informed and we are holding their feet to the fire and making them accountable for their actions. No more back room deals. I'm taking a front row seat. Can't wait to watch the movie.

I wrote on Facebook today, something I rarely do. I just wanted to say thank you to the people of Massachusetts for their common sense. One of our liberal friends, who live in the DC area, wrote on her Facebook that the people of Massachusetts disgust her. Disgusted? She may not agree with the outcome, but disgusted? I wasn't disgusted when President Obama won the election. Disappointed yes, but not disgusted. I want to write her and ask her to leave the DC bubble for a while. Come to "fly-over country" and get a taste of what middle and southwest America and the rest of the nation are really experiencing.

Grasshopper's Diary: February 4, 2010

I was thinking if I ever went to a town hall where O was speaking, I would ask why he puts down the TEA Party people. I would explain to him that I am not racist, in fact I would tell him that my best friend is black, and when people think that is a cliché, I would also say he is my husband. I would let him know that I am not a right-wing extremist, I'm just an average American who has never been politically active but has a need to implore Washington to quit spending, quit lecturing and to follow the Constitution. Why does he as President feel a need to call us out? Isn't free speech allowed in a free country?

I do not agree with your ideology, Mr. O, and I have the right to say so. That does not make me a racist, nor an extremist, nor dangerous. What is dangerous is being demonized by those in authority. That, Mr. President, is dangerous.

Grasshopper's Diary: February 10, 2010

Ok, you know how much I like Sarah Palin. She was the keynote speaker at the TEA Party Convention this past weekend, and she had written some notes on her hand. Ok, maybe she should have used note cards, but I get it. I would write on my hand. In fact, I have written on my hand before to help jog my memory. What's funny about writing on your hand is once you've done it, you always remember what's written on your hand.

Ok, back to the issue at hand... no pun intended. So yesterday, Robert Gibbs, the press secretary and White House spokesperson, writes on his hand: eggs, bacon, bread, hope, change... and shows this to the media thinking he's so funny just after the President said he is trying to be bipartisan. First of all, how 3rd grade acting is Gibbs? No disrespect to 3rd graders, and way to stay in the framework of bipartisanship. You know the more you make fun of Sarah, the more I like her. The "fly-over" states get what she is about. I know I'm just speaking off the cuff with this journal of mine, and it may sound un-intellectual (is that a word?); however, we are not stupid, and just because I'm not an elite, doesn't mean we (the people) don't know what is good for ourselves and our children. Live in your Washington, D.C. bubble the way you want, but let us do the same.

Oh, I've got to tell you, my dear husband sent me roses on Monday for Valentine's Day so I could enjoy them all week. He rocks.

Grasshopper's Diary February 16, 2010

Healthcare seems to be at the forefront again for the White House. Why, oh why, is this so important if the people do not want it? It's not about healthcare, is it? This should be on the back burner and it's on the front burner. Weird.

Watched the Olympics last night. Pair ice-skating. I'm not that interested since no Americans are in the running. Lots of falls last night. One thing I don't like about figure skating is that it is subjective. That's why I love downhill skiing, or luge, etc., as the clock picks the winner. That's why I like track and field. I like concrete facts not subjective emotions. Maybe that's why I am a conservative.

I read today on Glenn Beck's website that he had dinner with one of the richest men in the world. This man is just starting to figure it out, according to Glenn. This man thinks we have about a year before the SHTF (s%&! hits the fan). Glenn wishes he could reveal who this guy is, and he also said this man probably has never voted the same as Glenn. But he is now scared. He is more worried for the average man than for himself. All the people that work for him, etc., are all going to be in trouble. We as a country need to learn to become independent instead of dependent. Thank God I'm married to Ant. He started planning for independence about a year ago. Food, water, gold, ammo, and guns – it sounds crazy, huh?

Trust me…. it's not. It will be interesting to see what a year brings. Look at what is happening in Greece. That country has a huge debt problem and they continue to pay out more than they take in. Sound familiar. Watch Greece. It will become apparent where we are headed.

Grasshopper's Diary: March 9, 2010

Oh man, it's been almost a month since I have written anything in my journal. Honestly, I just didn't want to. I am so tired of what is going on in this country that I just wanted to not think about it, and just be. Sometimes, you just feel like giving up. I'm hearing the same thing over and over. The healthcare bill keeps rising from the ashes and being forced down our throats, and I just got tired of hearing about it and just wanted it to all go away. But, you have to keep fighting and debating and praying for our country.

I got mad at Ant last night. Kind of stupid, really never happens. It was 9:30 pm before he called me last night and, once again, I assumed he was dead. He was on the phone with his best friend, Lex, talking about what is going on in our country. Lex is starting to feel that something isn't right. And that's good. So, Ant had a great conversation with him. But he still could have taken my call, told me he was on the other line with Lex. We are not in the 1960s where you never knew who was calling on the other line, for God's sake. I was fine after I talked with him and he apologized. I just hate going straight to death. It's exhausting.

Grasshopper's Diary: Wednesday, March 24, 2010

Nothing is more important than our liberty and our freedom. So, I will go to town meetings, I will continue to read, I will be active in the TEA Party movement. Ant and I have been to quite a few in NM with everyday people who are sick and tired of the way things are being run in Washington. I write and call my Congressmen monthly, and I will actively campaign for any true conservative, and against those who aren't. Ant works, I work and travel weekly, but we are going to do everything we can to get out this message. Ant is a thoughtful speaker and a very good listener and truly understands the Constitution. Even if we lose, I will not have sat on my hands idly doing nothing. I do this for my child and for your grandchildren, because it is the right thing to do. Funny, my adopted child will do well under a cradle-to-grave government, but that's not what made this country great. Individual rights and limited government made this country great. The greatest on earth.

Grasshopper's Diary: March 24, 2010

So, let's just follow the evildoers into the abyss. I am not frightened of the end of times, but I am frightened of not fighting for what is right. I will fight to the end of times against those who want power and control over the people. My eyes are open and I walk without fear, but with resolve. Enslavement, under the pretense of what others claim is good for the whole, is corrupt. God gave us free will for a reason, and I'll be damned if government is going to take that away from me. Remember what I said about unalienable rights, which were given to us by our Creator. In essence, the government cannot take anything that your Creator bestows upon you away. Listen to these politicians speak. "We are doing this for you," they say "and for the good of society."

Eventually, redistribution of wealth makes everyone equally poor, much to the delight of our politicians. Redistribution of healthcare won't make the care any better. In fact, just the opposite will occur. We all will be equally less cared for, again, much to the delight of the political elite.

Grasshopper's Diary: April 6, 2010

Ok, this is just crazy. Obama is pushing for no nuclear weapons, not even for defensive purposes. I mean, I'm all for kumbaya, but that is not the real world. He has a duty as Commander-in-Chief to protect the citizens of the United States of America — to defend her citizens and protect the Constitution. This man is doing neither. I don't understand why people are blindly following him off the cliff like lemmings? Ant always said that what makes us different in having nuclear weapons is that we use them as a deterrent. They are never to be used as an offensive weapon, but only as a defensive weapon. If you attack us, we will use force and destruction against you. Not our President. We are all going to be sitting around the campfire singing while our enemies destroy us. Everyone needs to just back off from the race card and look at what this man is doing. His actions, not his color, his fricking actions! People are so focused on race that they can't see the forest for the trees. I truly fear for this country. Wake up America!!!

Side note: I also read today that stuck in the massive healthcare bill that most Americans do not want, is a provision where the President can build a healthcare corps... what? Can you say brown shirts?? Why in the hell do you need a healthcare military corps? I'll keep my eye on this.

Grasshopper's Diary: April 28, 2010

We have said there is going to be civil unrest on a multitude of topics...government spending, taxation, immigration, energy... so now we have the TEA Party versus the immigration amnesty promoters, which have now risen to the top of the news cycle because AZ signed into law their immigration bill, which actually mirrors the federal bill that our government isn't enforcing. Enforce the law, for Pete's sake! Protect our borders. Until that is done, this is going to be a volatile subject.

Grasshopper's Diary: April 28, 2010

Team Obama called out a SWAT team in full riot gear to protect the public against the Iowa TEA Party. Really, I know. It's crazy. Those grandmas singing God Bless America can get pretty rowdy. I wonder what the SWAT team was thinking. Scary, huh! Seriously, full riot gear?

Grasshopper's Diary: May 5, 2010

I read today where the President of the United States actually called us TEA Party activists, "tea-baggers," seriously? This man has no class... and isn't he the one that always preaches civility. Of course, every Tea Party I have been attended has been civil. Calling me a "tea-bagger" is rude and immature. Hmmm... makes you wonder why we don't have a grown-up in the White House. If you don't agree with his ideology, he is going to discredit you... pure Saul Alinsky tactics. Can you imagine if GW had discredited the Dixie Chicks? Instead, he said they have the right to say what they said. O name calls... and he's civil? Yeah, right.

Grasshopper's Diary: May 6, 2010

The stock market plunged 700 points today. Can you say "Greece?" We are doing the exact same thing Greece is doing – spending more in entitlements than we bring in. Something has got to be done about that. Chris Christie, the new governor of New Jersey, is having the same problem and he is asking the teacher's union to freeze their pay. That has caused quite a stir. I think I like Chris Christie. Let's see how this pans out. Why do we now have a country of entitlement types? Get this, Reverend Al "I love to race bait" Sharpton, said that he wants all households to be equal. Well, how about you start with yourself, Al? I suggest you divide up all your earthly belongings with, let's say, 10 of the downtrodden, no – make it 1,000 of the downtrodden. Hell, put me on that list, and let's all be Sharpton equal. Have fun with that, Al.

Sparring with Liberals

As Grasshopper and I became more active in our TEA Party support, we started to have more conversations with some of our liberal friends and family. Frankly, this isn't a very good idea. If you intend to remain friends with your commie, socialist, tyrannical, wealth stealing, bleeding heart Liberal friends or family, discussing politics from a conservative perspective is a really bad idea.

Case in point: I have (or had) several long-time friends who live in California. During this period of enlightenment for me, as early as 2009, I happened to have an e-mail exchange with one of them about Obama's socialist tendencies and tax-the-rich rhetoric. My friend responded that she saw Obama's election as significant as Nelson Mandela of South Africa. She also stated that while she didn't endorse bailouts, she didn't mind giving the government a little more of her money, if it helped someone in need. Well, isn't this always the Progressive mantra – it's okay for the government to take from some people to give to others who are in need. I pounced on her like a rabid dog and provided the following response:

> First of all, I don't take offense or see any disrespect if one has a view that disagrees with mine. One of the reasons I send out my opinions is that I want to be proven wrong and/or shown the flaws in my line of thinking. That's what dialogue is all about and while I may not always agree, I am at least willing to keep an open mind and listen to alternative views. That's what makes America, America!! Freedom of speech is fundamental to life, liberty, and the pursuit of happiness.

> Having said that, I must admit that I was shocked by your response to me and I want to pursue

your line of thinking and expand on the potential consequences of that particular way of thinking. First of all, I do not want to impugn your emotional side... I recognize that you are a caring person who has a soft-heart for the downtrodden and the disenfranchised. There is nothing wrong with that and we all should be as caring. However, where we disagree is defining the best way to take care of people who fall in that category.

Let's start with a couple of quotes that I think are illustrative of the viewpoint you espoused. The first quote is: "From each according to his abilities, to each according to his needs." The second quote is: "A government which robs Peter to pay Paul will always have the support of Paul." The first quote comes from Karl Marx (the founder of communism) where he believed that the ultimate goal is to strip man of their natural character and subjugate them to the power of the united individuals.

The second quote comes from George Bernard Shaw, a devout socialist, who made that quote not as a warning, but as a strategy to gradually coerce a country to move from democracy to communism. Now think about that for a second... if the government can make more people dependent on the government (create more Pauls), eventually, there will be fewer and fewer Peters to pay for the Pauls and ultimately, everyone will be dependent on the government (communism will reign supreme and the power will be with the political elite).

So the argument here is not one of Democrat versus Republican. The issue is whether you prefer individual liberty relying on one's self-interest as a motivating factor, or you prefer state control where the collective interest is the driving motivating factor. That's the issue that everyone is really up in arms about. From what you said, it sounds like you are a 'statists' and that it's okay for the state to take from you "according to your ability" and to give it to someone else "according to their need" (as determined by the state). If that is true, then my next question to you is if the state was currently controlled by Bush and not Obama, would you be as agreeable to the state's decisions to take your earnings and apply them for the collective good? Think about that possibility... your current trust in the "promise" of Obama is short-sided, because at worst, he will be in power for only eight years, and at best (if he continues his current policies), he will be removed after his first term. Then you will be at the whim of the next "leader" whether you "trust" him or not.

My next question to you is, given that you feel so strongly about sharing your wealth, you have the complete option, right NOW (without government intervention), to take your existing income and give half of it to a homeless person or an unemployed family. Are you presently doing that? Why not? Better yet, divide your income by 10 and help out 9 other families. This way you will each be equally wealthy even though YOU did all the work. How long are you willing to do that to support the other 9 families when they aren't working as hard as you? My guess is not very long, because there is NO INCENTIVE to work harder. And THAT, my bright lady, is the flaw in socialism. It is not Utopia, (although everyone has free health care and free food to eat). I don't recall hearing about anyone in America running to Cuba or the former Soviet Union to be taken care of, so why do you believe it will work now, here in America? It won't. Socialism has been proven to be a recipe for social mediocrity and ultimately, a failed system.

Let's look at the attempts where the U.S. has tried socialistic programs. Let's see, Social Security? Supposedly it should be available for each of us when we reach 65. Well, the system is already broke and the Ponzi scheme has worked for only one generation (our parents). Three or four years ago, the state of Massachusetts created a state-run health care system where 97% of the citizens have health care. It also is now broke, and they may have to end the system, because the state can't pay for it. Medicaid? Broke. In fact, I defy you to name ONE government program that is successful by private industry standards (i.e., it runs efficiently, it makes a profit, or at least pays for itself, and it is something we all use). Hmmm... Amtrak? Broke. The U.S. Post Office? Broke and losing more money (the U.S. Post Office is expected to lose $7 billion this year). Are you getting my point? Government can't run anything efficiently.

Finally, just do the math. You can't add 47 million people (supposedly uninsured) to the patient roles, keep the same number of doctors, fix total costs at today's current rate, and not expect health care quality to go down, access to be reduced (waiting lists), and government rationing to occur.

Listen, you don't have to believe me, but look at Cuba, Spain, France, Great Britain, and Canada. They have national health "scare," and all of those with the means come to America for serious health concerns, because we have the best system in the world.

Other than being elected, President (which by the way, is no small feat), what has Obama accomplished that ranks him in your eyes to the level of Mandela? Let's see, he has approved a stimulus bill that has quadrupled the country's deficit in his first 6 months of office (currently at $1.8 trillion). He has assigned over 40 Czars to report directly to him, circumventing the Constitutional checks and balances by ignoring his Cabinet members (look it up and ask yourself what they are doing?). He has supported the bailout of insurance companies, major banks, auto companies, etc., and placed government oversight employees to watch out for "us." Sounds like a government takeover of all of these industries. This will have major implications 2-3 years from now. Trust me, when inflation hits (and it WILL, due to the current devaluation of the dollar), none of these politicians will accept the *blame for their actions today... mark my words. They will blame the oil companies, the food industry, the utilities, etc., when prices start to become outrageous... and no one will recall that it was the decisions being made today that created this mess.*

You are an intelligent person. My plea to you is to stop being an idealist. Start paying attention, start reading, and watch other news channels besides NBC, CNBC and CNN. I can offer suggestions to get you started, but knowledge is key and staying in the "infatuation zone" with Obama (like the current mainstream media) is not the answer. He is doing more damage to this country than you can possibly imagine. Don't forget, I'm a registered Democrat, a black male, and I donated $500 to Obama early in his campaign. Then I started to pay attention and what I learned was not what I wanted for this country. He is exactly what he espouses to be, a political "statist" interested only in bankrupting this country for the "collective good." Stop listening to his words, and start paying attention to his deeds and of those around him.

I personally choose individual liberty motivated by self-interest. I oppose tyranny by any means, and I personally believe in self-reliance, personal responsibility, and hard work – words that you never hear coming out of Obama's mouth. He promises to take care of all of us. I don't want what he is selling.

Sorry this sounds harsh, but it is time to wake up. Capitalism is not the enemy! That's what makes us great! This country invented the airplane, personal computers, the iPhone... innovation and entrepreneurism and the knowledge that you will be rewarded when you put in the effort is the spirit of America. Companies that make huge profits, employ hundreds of thousands of employees who pay the bulk of the taxes that the government uses to support the welfare programs you want to maintain. You need to understand that the government is not a provider, it is a consumer. Worse than that, think of the government as a leech sucking the lifeblood out of the economy. It does not provide anything of value to the host, it only takes for its own survival. Eventually, if the leech grows too large, the host will perish. We are perilously getting close to that level now.

So let's talk about the cap and trade energy bill recently passed by the House of Representatives? Do you understand what that is about? Supposedly, this bill was created to limit carbon emissions to reduce the impact on climate change. Well, that's just fine and dandy. None of us wants to negatively impact the climate, do we? Except, if you notice, no one ever talks about global warming or global cooling anymore, because there is enough scientific data pointing to the fact that climate change is cyclic in nature (warming and cooling) and carbon emissions have an insignificant impact on the world's climate. (I'm sorry, but Al Gore won't debate this issue with any of the scientists who oppose his view. Just ask him and he will say the debate is over). Well it's not. But let's look at motive…

Cap and trade is about the government putting a cap on carbon emissions from various industries. If you are below the cap, you can sell your surplus to a company that is above the cap. By the way, Wall Street loves this because firms like Goldman Sachs can make money on any transaction (like selling and buying stocks). They receive a fee either way, except in this case, they are trading in carbon emissions. Wall Street wins, and the consumer (you and I) get screwed, as does anyone who uses energy (all of us), or any industry that uses energy (every business that I know of). These businesses will have to transfer the additional costs to us. Hmmm, just another way to get in our wallets. I'm sorry, but this is a scheme to soak us. We shouldn't focus on climate change, that's the ruse. We should focus on energy, getting more of it and as much of it as possible. Alternative energy is great, let's do it! But while we wait for the technologies to mature, let's pursue existing sources like near-by offshore oil resources, coal, shale oil, and natural gas. All of these are within our borders and we do not have to send billions of dollars to countries that despise us like Iran, Venezuela, etc. Why aren't we pursuing this line of thinking? This country could easily be energy independent within 10 years given a concerted political effort to do so; but, we have a "green agenda" that isn't interested in national security or energy independence. They are more interested in telling everyone what kind of energy to use... solar and wind is good, gas and coal are bad. Screw that, I want whatever turns my lights on in the morning, as long as I don't have to pay more for it. By the way, the 'greenest' energy source this planet has to offer is nuclear energy. It is nearly infinite in supply, technology has been advanced to the point that fuel rods can be recycled, it has NO carbon emissions, and it has been operating in France for the last 40 years and provides 70% of that country's energy needs. Have you ever wondered why France is never in any oil or natural gas disputes? They don't give a damn! They produce all the energy they need. We could too, but the liberal media is too lazy to learn and understand the technical issues that would support nuclear power.

So, back to the "cap and trade" scheme. There is a company called Generation Investment Management, a private equity fund chaired by former U.S. vice president Al Gore. It just so happens that he acquired a 9.5 percent stake in Camco International Ltd, a carbon asset developer. Generation, set up in 2004 by Gore and David Blood, former chief of Goldman Sachs's asset management arm, at one point held 16 million Camco shares. Camco, which has one of the world's largest carbon credit portfolios, works with companies to identify and develop projects that reduce greenhouse gas emissions and then arranges the sale and delivery of carbon credits.

So you think it's about climate change? I call bull crap on that. It's about government and Wall Street financial firms' control of resources. If they need more money from the populace, all they have to do is lower the "cap" and more companies get taxed and the more consumers must pay. If you are a politician, this is a great way to maintain power and subjugate the citizenry.

Listen, I'm not some conspiracy nut job, but if you don't know what's really going on, you can be easily deceived. The current administration and our friendly Congress are attempting to deceive all of us. I implore you, don't buy into the rhetoric! All I ask is that you pay attention and question everything. That's the American way.

'nuff said...

I gladly await your response.

Anthony

As you might expect, my friend was none too pleased with my diatribe. Her response was:

Hi Anthony -

Well, I don't think my short e-mail was meant to cover the details of how I thought things should happen, just show the tendency of my thinking. I don't agree with repaying irresponsibility, but I do agree with helping those in need. How that happens I don't have the qualifications to say, but as I understand the current push in health care reform, part of the cut in costs is coming from the health care industry charging less. I have to leave the details to the politicians who are elected purportedly because they know these things, and for whom we voted to represent us.

Anyway, I'm not going to haggle over issues. I don't have the stomach for it, and I regret having expressed my opinion in the first place. Furthermore, your tone is arrogant, condescending, and insulting. Palin called Obama a terrorist, and I'm not sure what you are calling me. The two of you deserve each other.

Take care,

K

Well I couldn't leave it alone, I continued to push. I replied with the following:

First of all, you should never apologize for your feelings. Your response is emotional. Mine is based in facts. If you find the truth hurtful, I'm sorry. Why are you bringing up Sarah Palin? I didn't mention her in my response to you and I didn't call Obama a terrorist. The only thing I called you was a statist, and I defined what I meant by that. Statist isn't a bad word, it's a point-of-view. Just one I disagree with. All I ask is that you look at what Obama is promising.

Maybe my tone was strong, but that's because this is important to me. The country is important to me, and I have spent my life in the national security arena to protect this country. I'm sorry you saw it as arrogant, condescending, and insulting. Facts hurt. That was not my intent. I'm passionate about this and the only thing I can do is try to educate my friends and others, including myself, about what's happening. We each must choose our own path. I refuse to let this just happen to me without putting up a fight. My fight is not with you. It's with those politicians (including Obama) that I don't trust.

Well, this was her final response back to me:

Oh, please. "Facts hurt." That is your opinion, your point of view. They are the way you interpret things, not absolutes. Please stop talking to me like I am an idiot.

Oops. I may have crossed the line. You think? Okay. We didn't speak for some time after that. I told you it is a bad idea to discuss political issues with Liberals. Especially if you disagree with them. Since I use to be one, I know how they think. Pulling them out of the "we care for the down-trodden" rhetoric is difficult. Their emotions get in the way of logical thought. It's a tough sell convincing liberals. Notice that she considered facts as a point-of-view and not an absolute. How do you argue with anyone that won't accept a fact as is?

Here is a typical argument with a Liberal:

Conservative says - Four is greater than Three.

Liberal replies - That's only because Four comes after Three. If Four came before Three, Three would be greater.

Conservative says - But Four comes after Three.

Liberal asks - Why do you hate Three? Three works harder and always shows up before Four. Four isn't special or any better than Three and should be treated equally. I think you are biased against Three. Do you treat One and Two the same way? Are you some kind of numbers Nazi?

Conservative sighs - Ok, you're right. To prove that your theory is correct, and that I'm not a numbers Nazi, I'm going to hand you three $100 bills as long as you give me the equivalent four $100 bills in return. Deal?

Unfortunately, sparring with Liberals sometimes sounds like the above argument. If you can't agree on the facts, you can make any argument sound logical and rational for the position you are taking. Liberals excel on not agreeing on the facts.

Grasshopper's Diary: March 23, 2010

Well, they did it. The Democrats used a Congressional gimmick called reconciliation and passed healthcare. I think our President is going to sign it sometime today. I am just furious. The will of the people be damned. I am pissed, but now my resolve is greater than it was before. Let's get these progressives out of office!

It's funny how the mainstream media discounts the people and demonizes the TEA Party movement of which I am a part. I am seeing reports today from the MSM that the TEA party group in DC this past weekend was using the "N" word and that the only reason they hate this healthcare bill is because of the color of our President's skin... what? Well, that's the Saul Alinsky tactic. Just say it enough and it shall become true. TEA Partiers are racist, TEA Partiers are racist... see, it's almost true, isn't it? Unbelievable.

They did that to Sarah Palin too... say she is stupid enough times and it becomes true... just ask anyone that is not a Palin supporter. They won't say it's her policies, it's because she is stupid. When I ask for an example, I get the "she said she could see Russia from her front porch..." no she didn't, Tina Fey on Saturday Night Live said that. I may not yet consider Sarah ready to become President of the United States, but it's not because I believe she is stupid.

Now, on a personal note, Ant and I just got back from San Diego. Great time, but Lordy, California is expensive. We stayed near the Gas Lamp District, which was wonderful and close to everything. When we checked in, Ant and I walked in together and approached the front desk. I thought it was fairly obvious that we were together, but the female attendant asked me if I wanted a separate room. I told the lady, no, I sleep with him. And it's ok, because we are married.

I wasn't sure how to interpret her request. Was it just an honest mistake on her part, or was it some kind of hidden code for "Are you okay lady, do you need help? Are you being held captive by this black man?" Ok, maybe it wasn't that bad, but it was weird and funny at the same time. Later that evening, we went to an awesome restaurant-bar on the roof of the hotel. It was kind of techno-modern with a large outdoor fireplace where people could congregate and sit around. Toward the end of the night, a couple approached us and asked Ant if he played basketball or baseball. Of course, he plays neither, but because he is 6'3", black and married to a white woman, he must be an athlete, right? Personally, I think it's because he just looks damn good, but what do I know. Of course, I am assuming all this is going on in their head, which makes me no better than the person who asked if Ant was an athlete. When Ant went to the bar, I decided to play a game with this younger couple and I told them yes, he played baseball, but he is very private and doesn't want to talk about it. Plus, when he quit playing pro, he went back to school and got his PhD of which he is more proud. The couple bought the story hook, line, and sinker. Obviously, the baseball part of this is not real, but the PhD part is. However, it doesn't make for as good a story when playing make believe and you are out of town guests. It's not that I think his engineering job is boring, I know for a fact that it is not. However, to the general public, engineers are just flat-out boring!

Grasshopper's Diary: March 25, 2010

I sat beside a gentleman on the way to Albuquerque tonight. He was on his way home to California. He is a Barack supporter, and most of his support comes from his disdain of George Bush. My goal was to challenge him to not give Obama a pass just because of his dislike of George Bush. That is exactly what he was doing. I think I convinced him that it's not Bush vs. Obama, it is limited government vs. government control. I asked him to quit listening to what Obama says and watch what he does. It is about capitalism vs. socialism. He really listened! He believes in free market, etc., but is so mad at Bush that he can't see the forest for the trees. Listen, I was a Bush supporter, but now I understand that he was a Progressive as well. I don't think Bush understood that he was Progressive. Anyway, we had a very interesting conversation and the gentleman that was sitting near the window commented on our conversation as we were walking through the airport in Albuquerque. He said I just may have gotten this gentleman to think in a different way. I hope so... one person at a time.

Ant's Comments

Over the next couple of months, I think Grasshopper was beginning to watch too much Glenn Beck on the television. I'm speculating only because of some of her recent "end of the world" diary entries -

Grasshopper's Diary: May 11, 2010

I need an ax.

Grasshopper's Diary: May 12, 2010

I need matches.

Grasshopper's Diary: May 13, 2010

Today, Nancy, an assistant that works in our office on Thursdays came up to me and said that she doesn't ever vote because the politicians are just a bunch of hypocrites and it doesn't matter anyway. I told her it does matter. It matters for her children; it matters for generations after her. It is her right and her responsibility to vote. She began weeping. I didn't mean to make her cry. She knows in her gut something is wrong with our country and where we are headed, but she doesn't pay attention. I told her that no question is stupid and she has to start somewhere.

I suggested the first thing she should do is register to vote. I also suggested that she start watching Glenn Beck. As Ant says, "Beck is America's teacher." So start there. She says she is going to do that. She was also crying because she doesn't like confrontation, and she doesn't know enough to fight back. So, she is going to start learning, listening, and reading. I say good for her!!! I also told her that I think God is ALL INFORMATION, so the more you know the closer you get to God. She said she is embarrassed because she doesn't know a lot. I responded "Never be embarrassed, just ask me and I will try to point you in the right direction to get information." I know, I know, I'll be pointing her in the direction I think she needs to go. Facts are the answer. I will point her towards the facts. Facts are a hard thing to refute. I'm so, so proud of Nancy for speaking up.

Grasshopper's Diary: May 18, 2010

I need a tent.

Grasshopper's Diary: May 19. 2010

I was talking to Ant last night and I used a word that can only come out of my mouth. "cohese." I used this most excellent word as follows: Gretchen Carlson, the morning co-host on Fox & Friends, her personality doesn't cohese with the group like Alisyn Camerota does. Ok, ok, I know some form of cohesive or cohesion was what I was searching for, but I kinda like that word as a verb. You just wait, it will be in the dictionary one day... ok, maybe not.

[Note from Ant: Grasshopper is a great "coheser" with people, but not so much with words]

Grasshopper's Diary: May 20, 2010

We are going to Arizona for vacation. We decided to go on a "buycott." We want the people of Arizona to know that we support them. Our President and the President of Mexico trashed Arizona from the White House today. Unbelievable.

My husband and I are active in the Albuquerque TEA Party. We are not racist, we are not radical loons, but we will be quiet no more. Forced redistribution of wealth is theft. Years and years of hard work and saving our money, and suddenly our government decides what rich is? President Obama said there comes a time when people have made too much money... really? I wonder how much is too much. Obama made over $5.5M last year, is that too much? Is $100K too much? Where does it state the government has the power to decide how much money you get to keep?

How convenient is that for the government? They steal money from me to give to their chosen charities. I personally give to charity all the time. I give to my church, I give to a homeless shelter in Fort Worth, I give to breast cancer research, and the point is that I choose to give to the organizations I think are important. I believe it is important to give to your community... but by choice, not by coercion. Is it ok for a thief to break into my house and take what he thinks he deserves? Well, it's not the government's place to do that either.

Who is Our Pharaoh?

After the health care bill was passed, one of our neighbors sent us the following e-mail with the subject title: Lesson from 4,000 Years Ago.

(Note: This is a message from the Pastor of a predominantly black church in Virginia. Perhaps we should decide who our real leader is? It is amazing to see that very little has changed in 4,000 years.)

SERVICE -STIMULUS SERMON Genesis 47:13-27

Good morning, brothers and sisters; it's always a delight to see the pews crowded on Sunday morning, and so eager to get into God's Word. Turn with me in your Bibles, if you will, to the 47th Chapter of Genesis, we'll begin our reading at verse 13, and go through verse 27. Brother Ray, would you stand and read that great passage for us? ...(reading)...

Thank you for that fine reading, Brother Ray. So we see that economic hard times fell upon Egypt, and the people turned to the government of Pharaoh to deal with this for them. And Pharaoh nationalized the grain harvest, and placed the grain in great storehouses that he had built. So the people brought their money to Pharaoh, like a great tax increase, and gave it all to him willingly in return for grain. And this went on until their money ran out, and they were hungry again.

So, when they went to Pharaoh after that, they brought their Livestock - their cattle, their horses, their sheep, and their donkey - to barter for grain, and verse 17 says that only took them through the end of that year. But the famine wasn't over, was it?

So the next year, the people came before Pharaoh and admitted they had nothing left, except their land and their own lives. "There is nothing left in the sight of my lord but our bodies and our land. Why should we die before your eyes, both we and our land? Buy us and our land for food, and we with our land will be servants to Pharaoh."

So they surrendered their homes, their land, and their real estate to Pharaoh's government, and then sold themselves into slavery to him, in return for grain. What can we learn from this, brothers and sisters? That turning to the government instead of to God to be our provider in hard times only leads to slavery? Yes.

That the only reason Government wants to be our provider is to also become our master? Yes. But, look how that passage ends, brothers and sisters! *Thus Israel settled in the land of Egypt, in the land of Goshen... and they gained Possessions in it, and were fruitful and multiplied greatly."*

God Provided for His people, just as he always has! They didn't end up giving all their possessions to government, no, it says they gained Possessions! But I also tell you a great truth today, and an ominous One. We see the same thing happening today - the government today wants to "share the wealth" once again, to take it from us and redistribute it back to us. It wants to take control of Healthcare, just as it has taken Control of Education, and ration it back to us, and when government Rations, then government decides who gets it, and how much, and what kind. And if we go along with it, and do it willingly, then we will wind up no differently than the people of Egypt did four thousand years ago - as slaves to the government, and as slaves to our leaders. What Mr. Obama's government is doing now is no different from what Pharaoh's government did then, and it will end the same.

And a lot of people like to call Mr. Obama a "Messiah," don't they? Is he a Messiah? A savior? Didn't the Egyptians say, after Pharaoh made them his slaves, "You have saved our lives; may it please my lord, we will be servants to Pharaoh"? Well, I tell you this - I know the Messiah; the Messiah is a friend *of mine; and Mr. Obama is no Messiah! No, brothers and sisters, if Mr. Obama is a character from the Bible, then he is Pharaoh. Bow with me in prayer, if you will. "Lord, You alone are worthy to be served, and we rely on You, and You alone. We confess that the government is not our deliverer, and never rightly will be. We read in the eighth chapter of 1 Samuel, when Samuel warned the people of what a ruler would do, where it says "And in that day you will cry out, because of your king, whom you have chosen for yourselves, but the LORD will not answer you in that day." And Lord, we acknowledge that day has come. We cry out to you because of the ruler that we have chosen for ourselves as a nation. Lord, we pray for this nation. We pray for revival, and we pray for deliverance from those who would be our masters. Give us hearts to seek You and hands to serve You, and protect Your people from the atrocities of Pharaoh's government.*

In God We Trust... Amen.

Attributed to [Smith, 2009].

Chapter 6

THE DIARY OF A MAD WOMAN

1. **NASA's Mission:
   Make Muslims feel better.**

2. **Do Progressives care about minorities?**

3. **Only God can determine if we are still worthy.**

The summer of 2010 is when America started to see the true colors of the Obama administration. The mainstream media continued to serve as surrogate lap dog, cheerleader, and protective shield for the One. However, several cracks started to appear in the dam and despite the MSM's best efforts to hide the Obama agenda from the masses, the masses could tell that something was fundamentally wrong. The economy wasn't turning around, jobs weren't being created, and an overall malaise hung over the spirit of Americans. It felt like... Europe.

Hot Fun in the Summer Time

Grasshopper's Diary: July 11, 2010

I've been neglecting this diary for some time. Some of it has been downright laziness on my part, some forgetfulness, and some just lack of time. It has been an interesting month. Ant's mom, Ms. H has moved to Fort Worth and I live with her on the days I am working in Fort Worth. The interesting thing about this is my son, K, is working for Ms. H as her "go-for." He is helping her unpack her items, he runs errands to the store, he is her "let's go eat something" chauffeur, and an all-around companion. This is good for them both. I told Kevin he should start a company called Errands for Elderly. He always seems to get along with older people and he loves the one-on-one. It's less confusing for him. Confusion always leads to something not good for K, so this relationship is a blessing.

It has been tougher on me, but in a good way. Lots of driving, picking K up, checking in on Ms. H, etc., but the way I see it, both Ms. H and K are obligations I will endure, and I mean that in a dutiful way. This is my contribution to my marriage and to life in general. Ant does a lot of things well, one of them is his contribution to national security, but taking care of his mother in an emotional capacity is not one of them. He is, after all, an engineer. This is something I can do well.

On the political front, the world is upside down. This past week, the head of NASA, Charles Bolden, NASA's Chief Administrator was on Al Jazerra TV and said the following:

> "When I became the NASA administrator – or before I became the NASA administrator – he [Obama] charged me with three things. One was he wanted me to help re-inspire children to want to get into science and math, he wanted me to expand our international relationships, and third, and perhaps foremost, he wanted me to find a way to reach out to the Muslim world and engage much more with dominantly Muslim nations to help them feel good

about their historic contribution to science ... and math and engineering," Bolden said in the interview [Fox News, July 05, 2010].

What?? This is one of Barack's initiatives for the NASA program? Are you kidding me? The news media outlets where this was NOT mentioned include: NYT, Washington Post, ABC, NBC and CBS.

Then, the DoJ dismissed the case against the New Black Panthers (NBP) on their voter intimidation case in Philadelphia. The Obama administration won a default judgment in federal court in April, 2009 when the Black Panthers didn't appear in court to fight the charges. The administration moved to dismiss the charges in May, 2009.

One of the NBP was caught on a camera phone saying how he "hated the white crackers and that we should kill white babies." I guess black-on-white hate speech is not considered racism in Eric Holder's world, but if this had been reversed, it would have been all over the nightly news. And, rightly so. Again, none of this appeared on the front pages of the NYT, NY Post, or was a lead story on ABC, NBC and CBS.

Grasshopper's Diary: July 13, 2010

During June, Ant and I have been watching Glenn Beck's history on the Founding Fridays. These history-teaching events by Beck have been fascinating, but one of the best was on African American Founding Fathers. What? African American Founding Fathers?

We discovered that the Progressives have eliminated a lot of American history to fit their narrative. David Barton highlighted a book entitled *"The Colored Patriots in the American Revolution."* One of the little known facts about the American Revolutionary War was that a black man by the name of Wentworth Cheswell rode North as Paul Revere rode West during the midnight ride to alert defenders of the arrival of the British fleet. Because the British invaded and moved West, no one recalls the other rider. It should make all African Americans proud of this country if they understood the sacrifices and contributions made by many of these men.

Progressives. I believe they are intentionally destroying our country. They want to demonize the Founding Fathers, diminish the Constitution, and remove God. I have been reading a lot from David Barton, who is a fantastic historian and a wonderful teller of our history. He said there are four immutable principals of American government, and they are:

1. There is a Creator

2. He gives certain guaranteed unalienable rights to man (among which the Founders identified life, liberty, property, self-defense, right of conscious, due process, etc.)

3. Government exists primarily to protect and secure the rights that God gave man.

4. In social compact, below God-given rights and moral law, government is to be operated by the consent of the governed.

Every one of these four things is being stripped from our nation. Ant and I are going to a Glenn Beck function in August at the Lincoln Memorial. The theme is "Restoring Honor." I can't think of anything more important for future generations.

Grasshopper's Diary: July 14, 2009

I watched Glenn Beck last night and he talked about social justice being advocated from the pulpit. He also talked about the New Black Panthers. The head of the New Black Panther movement said they are going to be at Beck's Restoring Honor Rally. Uh-oh. I am slightly afraid being a mixed race couple and all. I say you can't let people intimidate you for what you believe is right. This is a rally about restoring honor in America. This is a rally to honor those who have served. This is not about race. This is about honor. Hatred is a horrible thing. We have to stand up for what is right. And this is right. One of the reasons I married Ant is because he is honorable and just. We will go to DC to promote those values. I am nervous, but remain vigilant.

Grasshopper's Diary: July 20, 2010

Yesterday I signed the non-violence pledge promoted by Glenn Beck. It's for the 8/28 Restoring Honor Rally. Martin Luther King promoted this during the Civil Rights movement. It is the right thing to do. I also took Beck's pledge to pray on my knees. Praying on your knees makes one a humble servant. I tried it last night and broke down in tears. It was a humbling and eye opening experience. God is truly the answer to get out of this mess.

We have a President who believes in collective salvation that has its roots in socialism. It is evil. Individual salvation is our path home. Salvation through government hardens the heart. Charity through your own giving warms the heart. Pledge to be honest. Honest with yourself, honest with those around you. Once again, we have a President who is not honest. He is a deceiver. For example, he said during the health care debate that health insurance mandate is not a tax, but in fact his attorneys are arguing in court that it is a tax. Pledge to be charitable. That starts in the home. Be charitable and kind to those in your family and charity will spread to the community. Faith, hope and charity. Thank you, Glenn, for bringing those traits to the forefront in my life. On a side note, Glenn Beck has macular dystrophy. God has a plan, and Glenn's heart is good. I pray for his recovery.

Grasshopper's Diary: July 23, 2010

Today is my 55th birthday! Woohoo! It is also the day that Ant and I are no longer the same age. Every March, we become the same age and every July I become a year older. I hate it.

Anyway, we had some friends over for fajitas and margaritas. I was telling Cruz, one of our liberal friends, about the rehearsal dinner my boss had for his son's wedding in Aspen, Colorado. It cost him a hefty sum. Cruz responded with "No wonder the rest of the world hates us." I thought to myself, "What? Just because my boss spent a hefty sum on a rehearsal dinner?"

First of all, my boss gives a lot of money to charities and organizations of his choosing. Secondly, others benefit from his spending of this money: the restaurant owner/employees, the food distributors, the local economy for bringing in tourists from out of town, etc. Thirdly, my boss earned his money, it is his to spend as he wishes. If this is why other countries hate us, so be it. That comment really blew my mind. Why do we want to be like other countries? My attitude - I would much rather be unequally wealthy, than equally poor.

Grasshopper's Diary: July 26, 2010

We are in trying times. And we are hearing the "racism" word ad nauseam. Shirley Sherrod (who works for the USDA) was filmed giving a speech at a NAACP meeting. She seemed to be saying that she did not give a white farmer "the full force of what I could do" after he asked for assistance.

However, the video clip was taken out of context. Sherrod stated:

> *"My point in telling that story is that working with him helped me to see that it wasn't a black and white issue." Sherrod admitted to the NAACP that she eventually became friends with the farmer and worked with him for two years to help him avoid foreclosure.*

This video was posted on a website called BigGovernment. com. Within hours of the video being posted, Ms. Sherrod was forced to resign by someone in the White House. The White House or the USDA did not bother to watch the entire video. They were frightened that Ms. Sherrod was going to be on Glenn Beck that evening. She was not. So, the MSM spins the story the next day that Fox News is racist because they showed the video out of context. Never mind that Obama's Administration fired her without due process. She was asked to resign before Fox News ever picked up the story. And it became a story because she was forced to resign. The MSM scream racist. It is getting old.

I am tired of the word "racist," especially because it has lost its power. I wonder, if I disagree with my husband, would I be considered a racist? [Note from Ant: The answer is yes]. Just because our president is black and I disagree with everything the man is doing, am I a racist?

Have you ever wondered if the Progressives in this country really care about minorities, especially blacks? Over 90% of blacks vote for the Democratic Party. The less than 10% are called Uncle Tom's, traitors to their race, or simply kowtowing to the "man." Really? No one asks those 10% why they didn't vote Democratic. That is because the Progressives are afraid the others will find out the truth. It is better to pull them back into the bucket "the crab mentality" than to let them be free. That's the tactic of the Progressives. It's no different than the slave owner who says he is nice to his slaves: he feeds them, clothes them, shelters them, and then the ones that try to escape by running away are traitors and must be punished for leaving the plantation as an example to those still on the plantation.

Don't demonize the slaves that got away, they are free. Free to make their own mistakes, free to feed, shelter and clothe themselves. Freedom is powerful. That's right,

Democrats, you don't want your slaves escaping the plantation. Your political power and future goes up in flames if you allow blacks to leave your plantation. The Progressives have torn apart the black family and made many blacks dependent on the government. That sounds like slavery to me.

Grasshopper's Diary: July 27, 2010

Ant and I watched this movie called *Diary of a Tired Black Man*. We thought it was going to be a comedy and it turned out to be about the relationships between black men and women and their perceptions of each other. The movie highlighted how many children in the black community have grown up without a father figure; it showed how the women left behind refer to those black men as scumbags; and it depicted the negative impact these black women have on their children when they reflect their personal views of black men toward their own children. The movie's premise was interesting and not at all what I expected.

The one thing it made clear to me is that the government wants people on its plantation. Our government wants to be your "father" who takes care of you and your family. Seriously, tell me what have 50 years of welfare done for the black community? Conservatives want to get you off the plantation. I'm so tired of the word "racist." So very tired.

Grasshopper's Diary: July 28, 2010

I am so looking forward to Glenn Beck's Restoring Honor Rally. Interestingly enough, he said not to bring any signs, as that

143

is what the media will show, and if there are impostors in the crowd with ugly signs, we will know whom they are. Pretty clever. The media is still out there saying TEA Party type people are racists. Oops, there is that word again. Are there racists in the TEA Party? Probably. I personally have never met one. Are there some racists in the NAACP? Probably. Are there racists in the Democratic Party? Probably. That does not diminish the cause for which each group stands. I am not a racist, and I will no longer be silent. Let the media call us names, I am not going away. And that, my dear friends, is what scares them.

Grasshopper's Diary: August 5, 2010

This is the question that Glenn Beck asked last night: Are the events that are happening in Washington, DC benefitting you or them? Who has to play by the rules, you or them? Who pays for the spending, you or them?

TERM LIMITS. It doesn't matter whether you are a Democrat or a Republican, both parties are about power and control. Washington, DC is bulging from power, and we are suffering for it.

Guess what? The *NY Times* [Bai, 2010], placed a correction in their paper citing that "...there is no evidence that epithets reportedly directed in March at Representative John Lewis, Democrat of Georgia, outside the Capitol, came from TEA Party members."

Wow, I didn't see that publicized in the MSM news shows. It's funny to me that Nancy Pelosi and some members of the Black Caucus decided to walk through the TEA Party crowd instead of their usual route inside. Their excuse was that it was a beautiful day. Sure. They were either hoping for some kind of altercation, or they just wanted to gloat over their tyrannical healthcare mandate. The TEA Party crowd didn't behave like leftists. There was no violence, except for "Kill the Bill" exclamations from the crowd. So, the media had to make up an altercation. Racism! Racism! Racism!

I don't know if I wrote this earlier, but Ant has been asked to speak at the Albuquerque TEA Party event this coming September. I admire him so. He is taking a stand.

Grasshopper Diary: August 17, 2010

We are leaving next week to go to DC for the Restoring Honor Rally hosted by Glenn Beck. This is a non-political event that pays tribute to America's service personnel and other upstanding citizens who embody our nation's founding principles of integrity, truth and honor. I believe it will be much more than that; it will be about getting right with God. This nation is in trouble, and the only way to save her is to get back to God. I think this rally will be historic. We have been asked not to bring any signs, so we can single out those who are trying to portray this rally as racist. We've heard that the New Black Panther Party will be there and their goal will be to provoke violence. We have all taken a non-violence pledge that Martin Luther King, Jr. had his marchers sign back in the 1960s. In fact, MLK's niece will be standing with Glenn Beck on that day. This country is worth fighting for, but she can only rise from the ashes if we have God standing with us. I know you won't hear about this event on any of the news channels, so we will video the event. Rome is burning and the media is on the sidelines with their pompoms.

November, 2010 can't come fast enough, but I am of the opinion that the election is not the answer. The President and his wife are taking lavish vacations and he continues to play golf while Rome continues to burn (saber rattling in Iran, the economy continues to tank, the wars continue in Iraq and Afghanistan, lack of border security, rising energy prices, the national debt, the deficit, etc.). Only God can determine if we are still worthy.

Grasshopper Diary: August 18, 2010

I came across this article on REDSTATE.com posted by Janis entitled: "It's Time This Was Said - And I'm Saying It" - which struck me for its timeliness. In the article, Janis offered up a prayer for this country [Janis diary, 2010]:

> "Dear God, who is the Father of us all, please forgive us our human sins and omissions. For too long, too many of us have thought that we alone were capable of taking care of things here on earth. Yes, I know that must give you heartburn and a rueful smile, but that's what we thought. And here we are, come to a pretty pass indeed.

> "Your chosen people, Israel, face certain doom if Iran is allowed to proceed with its evil intent. America, once the champion of freedom, prosperity, and equality for all, is now laid low by those who intend to wipe out her ability to champion anything of value in

your eyes. Where once this country acknowledged You as our spiritual source and inspiration, we are now faced daily with being told that to do so in public makes us enemies of the state and of the people as well. Where once we protected and cherished our young and the most vulnerable among us, now we are told that the rights of the state must come first. That to deny a person the chance to murder their young is discriminatory to their rights, and that to continue to protect those who suffer life with severe challenges is 'not productive.'

"We watch as the world descends ever further into poverty and chaos in so many countries, as those who would replace You with the power of the State work their will. All the time thinking that they have won, they have smothered Your words and Your influence from the people they tyrannize, giving them only the choice of their way or…. no way. This is happening here, too, Lord, and your people here need Your help to defeat this evil.

"While the human part of me wants nothing so much as some very well-directed lightning bolts, maybe a few limited plagues and locust swarms in the right areas, that is not my call to make. I will take my direction from the book Jonah in the Bible, who was so angry with God for not destroying Nineveh that he huffed off into the desert to hide from God. That didn't work out so well for him. He argued with God that God should never have sent him on a fool's mission to save Nineveh because he knew that

God would be all loving and forgiving and wouldn't destroy the place. Sure enough, that's what God did when the citizens followed their king's example and set about praying to God for forgiveness when faced with their destruction. Jonah was not a happy camper over this news. So, God made His point with Jonah by giving Jonah relief from the hot sun of the desert. Then He took it away. When Jonah got mad all over again at the death of the plant that shaded him, God moved in for the win. 'You are angry that the plant died because of the worm I sent to kill it, Jonah?' 'Yes, Lord, I'm angry enough to die over it!' 'But, Jonah, it's only a plant. Yet you would have me kill over 120,000 people and animals in Nineveh for their sins.' Well, it is not quoted in the Bible as such, but I would imagine that God's next remark had something to do with "What's wrong in this picture, Jonah?"

So I'm saying it here: We can plot, plan, and work all we want to get our country back from those who are hell-bent on destroying it. And we should do ALL those things as hard as we can. But, unless we offer our efforts up to God to use us as He will, then we will not succeed. Our Founders knew a thing or three about tyranny and about having the deck well stackedagainst them. But they knew even better who would make their efforts come to fruition and it was not the best candidate of all in the next election. It was God, and God alone, who could come through and bless their efforts with success. Why? Because they bowed their knees to Him and asked for that blessing.

"So, I ask for His blessing now on our efforts and hope that all who read this will do the same. And for our opponents in this, for all those who scoff at the notion of God the Father, the Almighty and His authority over us, this is my prayer for you:

"May all who God created know in their hearts and in the dark of the night, that they are His children. May they reach out and ask for His forgiveness and His mercy. May they seek to feel His grace in their lives and in their work. And may they turn from the evil that they do knowingly. May they once more be reunited with their own souls and do as God has commanded us from the beginning. Simply, to love one another as He has loved us.

"And for those who scoff at the very notion, I give you two examples– there was Nineveh, which was saved because the people listened and heeded the warnings that Jonah was sent to give them. And then there was Sodom and Gomorrah, which did not and was destroyed utterly. You have a choice. For those of us who believe as our Founders did, so do we.

Amen"

I too say Amen.

Election Season 2010

Grasshopper's Diary: August 25, 2010

Flying home early so I can get ready for the rally in Washington, DC. I am nervous, but so excited.

Grasshopper's Diary: August 27, 2010

Well, we are leaving today. Ant says we have nothing to fear. Go with a happy heart and we will be fine. We are flying on Southwest Airlines, the greatest airline in the business. As I was standing in line to get on the plane, I overheard the gentleman in front of me talking about going to DC for the rally. So, I told him we were going as well. It turns out that Charlie and Joni were a husband and wife team headed for the same event. They were so excited we were attending. Most of us really felt alone on this trek. Then the couple that sat in front of us on the plane was from Tucson and they were going, as well. In fact, they had been to the 9/12 TEA Party March last September and they were a plethora of information. It was strangely funny. At first, we didn't want anyone to know we were going. Then when we found out we were not alone, our courage began to rise. It's okay to talk about this country and our love for her. It's okay to talk about God, and to reflect back on our fundamental values. It was a great flight. We got to our hotel about 6:30 pm, ran over to Chop't Restaurant and picked up some salads and came back to our room to watch the event that Glenn Beck held in the Kennedy Center that night.

This was the night before the rally. I cannot tell you how blessed we were to have watched it. It started off with gospel music, and they sang "Mine Eyes Have Seen the Glory of the Coming of the Lord." Well right there at the beginning, Ant and I had tears in our eyes. David Barton (who I think must be the smartest American historian ever) and Glenn Beck hosted the event. The night was filled with men of God from all faiths. One of my favorites was a man named Dave Reeter (I think that was his name). This man was serving in Vietnam and a phosphorous grenade went off in his hand and literally blew him up. He is horribly disfigured, but his joy and love of the Lord just shines through. He was remarkable.

Then there was Rabbi David Lapin. Lapin spoke without a microphone, because Jews are not supposed to turn on electricity during the Jewish Sabbath. His talk focused on returning America to its roots in faith. He was hard to hear, but he must have been fantastic as the crowd erupted when he was talking. I got the gist of what he was saying... read the Bible and know it; make money, because if you make enough money for you and your family, charity to those less fortunate will follow; and pray for this country. Then Chuck Norris came out with his wife. He read George Washington's words, Thomas Jefferson's words, and Samuel Adams' words. Ant and I both held each other and cried. These were remarkable men who loved the idea of this brand new country. Read them. Know them. We go to sleep with comfort and excitement for tomorrow's rally.

Grasshopper's Diary: August 28, 2010

We woke up around 4:00 am and our plan is to walk to the rally around 6 am. The event starts at 10 am. We have chairs to sit in, a packed lunch, water, cameras and anticipation. As we are walking to the Rally, we met a woman who claimed to formerly be a die-hard Democrat, because she thought that Democrats were about helping the poor. At least that's what the nuns taught her. As an adult, she said she took a course in macroeconomics and a light bulb went off in her head.

She said she realized that the way the poor can get out of poverty is to create an environment that encourages wealth creation for all. Free enterprise. I'll have to ask Ant exactly what macroeconomics is to make sure I get it right.

We bid adieu to this lady and as we approached the Mall and headed toward the Lincoln Memorial, the crowd was getting thicker. It is 6:00 am and we find an open spot about halfway down the reflection pond on the right hand side, not far from a large projection screen. At 9:30 am, the entire reflection pond was filled with people on both sides and 3 times deep. We have no idea how many people showed up to the event, but what we do know is that we are not alone. Come to find out later that the estimate was around 500,000 people. I believe that figure. The crowd was packed from the Lincoln

Memorial all the way back to the Washington Monument. The mainstream media tried to lowball the estimate by saying only 87,000 people attended the event. The MSM cannot admit that the message promoted by Glenn Beck is resonating across the nation. They would prefer for him to just go away.

About 5 minutes before the Rally starts, three geese flew in formation down the center of the reflection pool. It was a "God" moment. I took it as the symbol of the Father, the Son and the Holy Ghost, but that's just me. Then about 1 minute before the event, an entire flock of geese flew down the middle of the pond barely skimming above the water. It was like God's flyover blessing this event. It was truly a great moment. Then it starts, the large screen showed a short video of cities, farmlands, and mountain ranges of this great country. We were asked to recite the Pledge of Allegiance. It was a great moment. We met many of those around us from all over the nation, Wisconsin, New Jersey, California, Texas, Michigan, New Mexico, Pennsylvania, New York, Virginia, Georgia... all in this one little area where we were located. The Beck rally allowed the world to see that America is full of honorable families, normal, sincere people of faith who just want the country to return to the magnificent vision of our Founding Fathers as expressed in the U.S. Constitution. Ant and I were privileged to be there. God is so good and He was so alive at this rally. I could go on and on, but I found this blog from The Central Texas 9-12 Project that says it all [Central Texas 9-12 Project, September 5, 2010]. In the blog, a woman brings her husband and two daughters to the Restoring Honor rally. During their journey home after the event, they ran into a black gentleman wearing an Obama tee shirt who had attended the opposing Al Sharpton "Reclaim the Dream" rally. However, this gentleman did attend a portion of the Glenn Beck rally, because Sharpton's folks told him that something nefarious was underfoot with Beck's rally. What he and his friends discovered was nothing remotely resembling what they were told. This black gentleman left the rally with a different perspective and mentioned to his daughters that "Glenn was something special..."

There is something good happening, and it begins with God.

Grasshopper's Diary: August 29, 2010

We had lunch with Kim and Everett in D.C. Later on we met up with Denice and had dinner with her. [See Anthony's speech in the Appendix to learn what happened]

Grasshopper's Diary: August 30, 2010

Flight home. After an emotional weekend, I get home and I'm watching television and this commercial comes on. The first scene is a Daddy pushing his little girl on a bicycle and she says "You can let go Daddy." Then that little girl is a grown woman at the altar, and she says "You can let go Daddy," and then the last scene is the same daughter holding her daddy's hand as he lies in bed as an old man, and she says "You can let go Daddy."

That deeply tugged at my heart. I miss my Daddy and I can remember saying at his bedside, "It's ok to let go, Daddy."

Grasshopper's Diary: September 21, 2010

Last night I shared with Ms. H, my mother-in-law, about Ant giving a speech at the Albuquerque TEA Party. She said that doesn't surprise her as Anthony's views are a bit crazy and skewed. What? I asked her why she felt that way. Of course, she had no answer and then stated she was tired and wanted to go to bed. I didn't pursue it, as Ant has asked me not to discuss politics with his mother because there is no changing her views. It is funny how liberals always have an excuse when they can't answer direct questions. Plump Jodi in DC said she was too drunk, Ms. H is too tired, ask any liberal for details and they will state they can't remember right now. If you are going to stand for or against something you should know why. Using the justification that our President is half-black is not an answer. That is an excuse.

Grasshopper's Diary: September 25, 2010

This is the day Ant gives his speech at the Albuquerque Tea Party. Ant named his speech "The Speech for Freedom." He didn't intend that name for external use, just for development purposes. Unfortunately, it got listed on the agenda with that name. Ant was laughing, as he thinks "The Speech for Freedom" has already been covered by the likes of Abraham Lincoln or Martin Luther King. Maybe Ant's speech is "A Speech for Freedom," but certainly not "The Speech for Freedom." I think he's being too critical of himself, but it did make us laugh.

Ant's speech was great (see Appendix). He had so many people come up to him and thank him for his perspective, and his honesty. The turnout for the event wasn't that great, but the people that were there were passionate. Afterwards, we

155

had about 20 friends come over for hamburgers, margaritas, etc. One of the couples that dropped by has lived off the grid for 10 years, but is back on it now. They are on my list of friends when "all hell breaks loose." We had a great time. All who stopped by were like-minded freedom lovers. Very cool.

Grasshopper's Diary: September 26, 2010

Today, a young black male from the University of New Mexico called to interview Ant regarding the TEA Party movement. Ant invited him to our house. Evan, about 20 years old, is a nice young man, who is clearly gay with an engaging personality. As I watch Ant from the kitchen being interviewed by Evan, I see a teacher and a student. Ant will explain why the TEA Party exists and what their purpose is in this political climate. He truly has Evan's attention. One person at a time... each one, teach one. Once you teach someone about freedom and liberty, it is hard to put out that fire. However, those damn Progressives are sure trying. We no longer will be intimidated, we will stand up and we will fight for what we think is right. I think I'll go fix Evan a plate of food so he can take some dinner home. I remember the days of being a poor college student and digging through my couch looking for change!

Grasshopper's Diary: September 30, 2010

I received the following e-mail from a friend of mine whom we met at the Restoring Honor Rally. I shared with him Ant's speech and he replied with the following comments:

"Hello Ant and Grasshopper,

"I just took a closer read of the fine speech that Anthony wrote and delivered. I was touched by your experiences in DC afterwards. The smugness of the plump couple in the restaurant was about right for a pair of Lefties. Believe me, I know many such. The silence of your friends is most moving. With my friends, I don't know which I resent more at this time, the silence or the occasional smug condemnation from those who are theologically against all judgment. Your silent friends were not just tone deaf and blasé towards what happened that day. They were against it and quietly seething, probably barely tolerating that you came all the way to DC to take part in it. Their quietness was likely a sort of politeness among those who do not want to dignify your trip and your enthusiasm with an argument, particularly one that they would likely lose. Nothing is more important to Lefties than maintaining self-esteem and feeling that he or she is on the side of the angels. When faced with a direct contradiction of their argument, which is their very essence, Lefties respond with sullen silence. Happens every time. Behind your back, they will say, "What happened to them? Did they just go over a cliff or something?" But what they will not do is honestly open themselves to the arguments you present.

"Interestingly, most of them see themselves as rational, modern people, not like those religious people, who seem driven by superstition. Religion, though, fills a need in every human soul. So, when one has discarded a faith, then another "faith" has to fill the void. Lord Chesterton said, "When people cease to believe in God, they wind up believing in anything." This is very true of our present secular modernist friends on the Left. They have dropped the patriarchal Abrahamic faiths under the banner of "Get your theocracy out of my democracy," and adopted another religion, that of political Liberalism. This faith, like all religions, deeply resents embarrassing questions, doesn't feel that it has to justify itself and casts all doubters as Heretics or "deniers." Believe me, this is true. As a religious person, I can spot a religion a mile away.

"So, their stony silence was a way to deny you the satisfaction, particularly as the event was organized by Glenn Beck. Again, most Lefties have never watched more than an occasional snippet of Glenn Beck and they certainly wouldn't understand his arguments about how apparently innocent Socialism can lead to totalitarianism. Meanwhile, most Liberals see only Nazism as a great evil. This is why they call everyone they disagree with a Nazi. They have never truly examined their side's fascination with Socialism and Communism. Although they will readily admit that Stalin was a bad guy, they *refuse to see the ideological connections with many Liberals and Communism or Communism's genocidal nature, before and after Stalin. To Liberals today and in the past, communism was just a false obsession of McCarthyism; not a real threat. These are people who responded to Rev. Wright's incantations with a big "So what?" They see the same with Anita Dunn and the rest of the neo-Marxist cast of characters that Obama has surrounded himself with. They simply cannot comprehend that there is anything wrong with it and, for someone like Glenn Beck who exposes it, they see him as the Antichrist – an emblem of philosophical intolerance best denigrated as a wing nut.*

"I have shed some tears as well for similar reasons, so I can well understand yours. Keep the faith, though. Literally.

AP"

This made me cry, but AP hit the nail on the head.

Grasshopper's Diary: October 14, 2010

I really think the theory proposed by Dinesh D'Souza in his book "The Roots of Obama's Rage" of the oppressed versus the oppressor may be accurate. It's the only thing that makes sense and explains the strange behavior of this Administration. I applied D'Souza's theory to the current Arizona debacle. If you believe that Barack Obama is anti-colonialist and that he believes the United States is the Oppressor, all of a sudden the Administration's actions toward Arizona make perfect sense. No wonder the Administration sued Arizona. He considers the illegal immigrants coming in from Mexico as the oppressed people. It just didn't make sense before, but now it does. That explains why other "oppressed" countries have joined our federal government in their suit against Arizona. Our sovereignty as a nation is not respected by this Administration. Unbelievable!

Grasshopper's Diary: October 19, 2010

The elections are 2 weeks away. I pray that good conservatives are elected and can stop this madness in our country. However, it is going to be a long, hard fought battle. If we lose, we get more of the same. Spend and taxation. If we win, we are going to be blamed for whatever goes wrong in the next 2 years, and a lot is going to go wrong. Glenn Beck asked two great questions last night on his television show, "Progressives are progressing to what? What is better than the Constitution?"

Grasshopper's Diary: October 22, 2010

I know a lot of people who listen to National Public Radio. I don't have a problem with that, but I do have a problem with my tax dollars funding it. It is a left-winged organization funded by my tax dollars. It is left leaning, and George Soros just gave NPR over a $1M to hire 100 journalists to attack Fox News. Some may think Fox News leans to the right, but at least your tax dollars aren't supporting it, and you can choose to watch or change the channel. Unfortunately, my tax dollars go to this pseudo-news organization and it angers me to no end. I feel similarly about the fact that the U.S. taxpayers fund the United Nations, another corrupt organization that holds America in contempt. The last straw with NPR is that they fired Juan Williams [Folkenflik, October 21, 2010], because of a remark he made about Muslims and that his comments were "inconsistent with our editorial standards and practices, and undermined his credibility as a news analyst with NPR."

So, it's ok to call the TEA Party participants "tea-baggers, racists, homophobes, and bigots," but it's not ok to say what Juan said. NPR should be defunded. My money doesn't need to go to such trash. If people want to find the same message as NPR, let them go to MSNBC and they can watch it with the other three hundred national viewers tuned to that channel. At least it isn't funded by taxpayer's dollars. I choose Fox News, but others don't have to pay for it. I have to pay for NPR. Hypocrites.

Grasshopper's Diary: October 24, 2010

I woke up in the middle of the night and couldn't go back to sleep. I worry about our country. I worry about the elections and fraud. I worry about freedom of speech being stifled. This is a very frightening time in our country. I truly do not understand why people choose government over individual liberty. I need to turn this worrying over to God. The best thing I can do is stay informed, continue to debate, and most importantly - vote. November 2nd can't come fast enough.

Grasshopper's Diary: October 27, 2010

Uh-oh, is it the beginning of civil unrest? I just got off the phone with Ant. Last week Ant stopped at the grocery store on his way home from work. As he was entering the grocery store this guy ran past him on foot with cans in his arms and stuff falling from underneath his jacket. Then Ant saw the store manager running out of the store chasing this guy. The bad guy jumped in a truck and immediately sped off. Ant got the license number and reported it to the store manager. He said it was surreal.

A week later, Ant was standing in line at the same grocery store. He said that he noticed a young woman, about 22 years old wearing a pink jumpsuit, standing in the express checkout line. Ant was watching her as she kept letting people go in front of her, which he thought was strange since she was in the express lane. Suddenly, he notices that she is heading for the store exit with her items in hand without paying.

Ant immediately told the cashier in his line what was happening and was informed that this type of occurrence is happening more frequently. The cashier stated that the grocery store rules are clear that once the person gets outside the exit doors, the employees are not to engage the thief - they have no recourse once they are out the door - for employee safety reasons. Clearly, this young woman was just waiting for the right time to leave. Either she was waiting for security to step away from the exit, or she had an accomplice outside in a get-away vehicle.

Wow. It's starting, and as our economy continues to suffer, it is going to get worse. Ant and I need to get our concealed carry weapon licenses and soon. We need to start carrying for our own protection. I hope none of what I think is going to happen happens. Keep the faith. I pray God has a plan.

Grasshopper's Diary: October 29, 2010

This is unbelievable. Bill Clinton has asked Kendrick Meek, who is a Black Democratic candidate for Senator in Florida, to drop out of the Senate race so that the Democrats would rally behind Charlie Crist (the Republican-In-Name-Only who lost to Marco Rubio in the primary). The former Florida Governor CC was upset that he didn't win the Republican primary, so he opts to run as an Independent. The Democrats are asking the Democratic black candidate to step out of the race. Are you fricking kidding me? Can you imagine if the Republicans asked their black candidate to step down so a white independent could win? Can you imagine the uproar from the Liberal press and the Black community? So, why is it that Democrats get a pass by the blacks all the time? Why? This is a joke.

Grasshopper's Diary: October 30, 2010

It's Halloween and Ant and I are in Las Vegas. I'm not sure, but I think this is the day that all young women who come to Vegas decide to dress up like sluts! It's like Mardi Gras without any guilt. Ant and I decided to go as Barack Obama and Sarah Palin again. Last year when we dressed up, everywhere we went people would say "Obama,

Obama, Obama." This year, it appears opinions have changed because it was "Sarah, Sarah, Sarah." It was great! I've included a picture from our Vegas trip.

Pretty darn good, huh?

Grasshopper's Diary: November 1, 2010

Tomorrow is Judgment Day. November 2, 2010, the day we take back America: The day we show both sides of the aisle that this is the people's government and they work for us, not the other way around. I am so tired of establishment Republicans and Progressives on the left. I'm tired of the elitist attitude in Washington DC. Tomorrow we take out the trash.

Grasshopper's Diary: November 2, 2010

I'm as nervous as a cat in a room full of rocking chairs. I got down on my knees this morning and prayed for an honest election. I wanted to pray for a win, but I know God doesn't work that way. If it's a fair-and-square election, then that's what I can live by. Ok, I can't stand it. Please, God, let us win tonight! Sorry, lost my head for a minute. Get back to you tomorrow when I know something.

Grasshopper's Diary: November 3, 2010

Stayed up as long as I could last night. I was thinking about taking some NoDoze to be able to stay up past 10. How pathetic is that? Nonetheless, went to bed with a smile on my face. We had a tsunami in the House races. A pickup of over 60 seats! My only disappointment was that the

Republican Congressional candidate from New Mexico lost to a left-wing Democratic candidate. I have no clue what is wrong with the people in Albuquerque. Why do they reward arrogance?

Speaking of rewarding arrogance, Senator Boxer won in California. You know, the Senator who wants to be called Senator instead of ma'am. And Jerry "Moonbeam" Brown won as Governor of California. California deserves what they get. If our Federal government even hints of bailing California out financially, I am going to throw a conniption fit. They voted for it, they must live with it.

My beloved Texas, O Texas, stayed true to her conservative values. So, Republicans, you go up there to D.C. and stand firm with your values. If not, we are having another election in two years.

Grasshopper's Diary: November 3, 2010

A long-time friend just hung up on me. My bad. I called him an elitist. I know better than to name call, so that's on me. But here's the rub, he believes that the TEA Party movement hurt the Republicans. Are you kidding me? It's the only reason they are not on the sidelines this time around. He said that Mike Castle might have won Delaware. I say, "At what cost." Mike Castle was a RINO at best. How could we know how he would vote? Cap and Trade – he may have considered voting for it. How can you consider Cap and Trade? I know for sure that Christine O'Donnell would not have voted for Cap and Trade. And to me, that's the whole point. Here's my email to him after he hung up on me:

"I apologize for calling YOU an elitist, but not for calling those In D.C. elitists. I stand firm on my positions, and I will not compromise. That's what got us into this mess to begin with. I will not side with the Olympia Snowes, the Lindsay Grahams, the John McCains and, yes, the Castles. I will stand firm with the Constitution and try to get those elected that believe in it. I do not play the party power game. I want people elected who will uphold the Constitution, nothing less. People like Senator Lisa Murkowski from Alaska irritate me. They think they are owed a seat in Congress - it's mine, and nobody can take it from me. Yes, I'm a TEA Party activist, and the Republican Party should be grateful. Without this uprising, the Republicans would be sitting on the sidelines. You and I will have to agree to disagree on this, but you shouldn't pick up your marbles and go home. Again, I apologize for calling YOU an elitist."

Grasshopper's Diary: November 10. 2010

I just got off the phone with Ant. He went to dinner with a former co-worker friend. One of the questions she asked him when the discussion turned to politics was, "What's the matter with Communism?" Ant said he was shocked that she could even ask that question, let alone not understand the impact or history of communism.

What's the matter with communism? Are you kidding me? Well, let's just start with the question "Where has it worked out well for the people?" Why would you want control and power in the hands of an elite few and not in the hands of the people? Why do you want the government to make decisions for you?

What is wrong with America? Do people not see that America is great because her power lies with the States and the people? Granted we have certainly strayed from the original intent, have we not? The Federal government is becoming our nanny. We the people are allowing it to happen. Where is our soul? Where is our spirit? The good news is that there are more people today who now understand the Constitution and our Founding Fathers and our basic principles. And that is a good thing.

By the way, Happy Birthday Marines!!!

Going home tonight. Yeah!! I miss my husband.

Grasshopper's Diary: November 24, 2010 –Thanksgiving

We have so much to be thankful for. Ant said he is especially thankful for the elections in November. Hopefully, this means America is awake. Over Thanksgiving, we invited our neighbors and their nephew, whom I just adore, to join us. We also invited the UNM student Evan and his boyfriend, Ted. Great kids. Well, I guess they aren't kids. Ted teaches at the local high school, so I guess I can't classify him as a kid. Evan is at UNM working towards his journalism degree. At dinner, we of course, talked politics. I think we have two new converts. Ted was convinced that Wall Street was the cause of the subprime problem without realizing the role government played in the whole process. He was very surprised. It certainly doesn't mean that Wall Street didn't take advantage of the rules, but our government set the rules. We talked about regulation and too much government intervention in our lives (the Patriot Act, the TSA pat down and naked machines). We talked about R and

D's being the same side of the same coin. We talked about socialism. We used the example for Ted that if he told everyone in his class they would get the average grade of all the students in his class, why would those who make A's even try. That made sense to him. Both Ted and Evan asked great questions. I think we had two converts by the end of the night. I gave Ted the book "The Creature from Jekyll Island" to read. We will have them back out to discuss further. Ant is such a good mentor and such a good teacher.

Dinner was great. Ant actually brined the turkey. Something we had never done before. Wow, does it make a difference. Nothing like good wine, good food, and a good discussion to make for a great Thanksgiving.

Chapter 7

ACTIVISM

The TEA Party Mission:

1. **A Constitutionally limited federal government.**

2. **A free market capitalistic system.**

3. **Fiscal responsibility and balanced budgets.**

The Occupy Wall Street crowd is a slick, well-oiled, AstroTurf group. I mean, really... who has time to party in Zuccotti Park for 30 days, complain about the top 1% of income earners, ask for free stuff while defecating on police cars, participate in public sex, and rape unsuspecting women? Is this a group you want to be associated with? Only if you are the President of the United States or a well-heeled Hollywood-type like Susan Sarandon, Michael Moore, and Def Comedy Jam producer Russell Simmons. The Hollywood elite represents the 1% the Occupiers claim to despise. Both sides are useful idiots. Conservatives should be careful and take them seriously. We understand their Saul Alinsky tactics and they will become more violent during the coming months, especially, if Barack Obama wins the 2012 election. Mark my words.

Joining the TEA Party

On April 15, 2009, I attended my first ever Tax Day rally in Albuquerque, New Mexico. Why? Frustration. I was tired of yelling at the television when hearing about our politicians' wasteful spending. I was frustrated with seeing my hard earned tax dollars being spent to bail out failed banks and businesses, and I was angry for sending letters to my progressive liberal Congressmen and Senators, only to receive a standard form letter back thanking me for contacting them regarding [pick your topic] and proceeding to tell me why they voted against my will. Personally, I understand that we are a representative democracy, a republic, and that one should not expect his or her representatives to agree with you on every topic. However, when the time comes that none of your representatives in Congress represent your views, your only recourse is to take to the streets in non-violent protest. The TEA party group did that for me. It helped me realize that I was not alone.

What is the TEA Party? In its simplest form, it is a loose affiliation of local and national grassroots groups who are fed up with the established Republican and Democratic spending policies from both parties. The TEA Party is not a political party although it claims representatives from the Republican Party, the Libertarian Party, and free-market Democrats, who are not socialists and are fed up with the political partisanship. Some claim the movement kicked off when CNBC news editor Rick Santelli criticized the government plan to refinance mortgages on February 19, 2009. He suggested holding a tea party for traders to denounce the banking bailout. The truth is that many of these local groups were already forming as a result of the Troubled Asset Relief Program (TARP), previously signed by George W. Bush on October 3, 2008. Santelli's rant may have served as a catalyst to the nation to rise up and let your representatives know that we do NOT condone this type of behavior from our representatives.

Each local TEA Party group has its own charter and value system, but in general, the mission and core values of the TEA Party are to promote and support:

- A Constitutionally-limited federal government

- A free-market capitalistic system

- Fiscal responsibility and balanced budgets

The goal of the TEA Party movement is to return political and economic power back to the states and the people and away from the federal government, as the original framers of the Constitution intended.

To me, this is simply resetting the country back to basics. However, the establishment Parties on both sides of the aisle initially ignored the movement. Nancy Pelosi had even gone so far as to call the grassroots movement "Astroturf." President Obama and many members of his Administration ridiculed the protesters in the hope that the movement would fade away as quickly as it began. When the ridicule did not work, charges of racism and attempts to assign all violent acts to the TEA Party protestors, and their supporters started to appear in the MSM. (Remember, claims of racism are just a tactic from the Left). None of the allegations were ever proven to be true. In fact, as Nancy Pelosi arrogantly marched through a TEA Party crowd carrying a large gavel to taunt the crowd on her triumphant passing of the Affordable Health Care Act, now referred to as Obama Care, the MSM made accusations that the TEA Party crowd had hurled racial slurs and spit at the Representatives as they went through the crowd. There were hundreds of protestors and press present during this event. Andrew Breitbart offered to pay $100,000 to the United Negro College Fund, if they could show any proof of such slurs or spitting occurring during the event. Two years after the offer, there are still no takers. Liberals lie and MSM supports the lie. Rule #2: *Don't believe everything you hear.*

Neither party really believed in the power of the TEA Party movement until the 2010 mid-term election, when the Nancy Pelosi controlled House of Representatives received a "shellacking," Princess Pelosi lost her majority throne, and the Democrats lost over 60 seats in the House. Now, the message of "cutting spending instead of increasing it, and reducing the size of government instead of expanding it" is starting to resonate amongst some politicians. However, there are still too many establishment Republican Congressmen and Senators that don't understand the mood of the country. Most Democrats are too far-gone at this point. It may take a few more election cycles, but the Progressives' time in Congress is limited and each will be replaced by a new type of conservative politician, one who runs to serve the country, not himself. Time is not on their side.

So, I became more active in the local TEA Party groups in and around Albuquerque. I started to meet more like-minded people who, like me, felt that the nation was on the wrong track. Grasshopper and I started to meet and socialize with friends and neighbors who had similar views to ours. While I continued to maintain my relationships with many of my Liberal friends, I found it more and more difficult to have meaningful dialogue with them.

Prior to the November, 2010 election, Grasshopper and I went to the 8/28 "Restoring Honor Rally" sponsored by Glenn Beck in Washington, D.C. Half a million Americans showed up to this historic event. While the MSM attempted to marginalize the event by calling it a "tea party," there were no political signs to be found and, hence, nothing the MSM could use to paint the event in a negative light. In fact, prior to the event, many MSM pundits attempted to slander the event with allegations of racism. Turns out, Dr. Alveda King, niece of civil rights leader Dr. Martin Luther King, Jr., and a cadre of men and women from all faiths and ethnicities were on stage and actively participated in the event. The MSM was wrong again. I was there. I left the event more inspired, more encouraged, and more determined to help this country return to its greatness.

On September 25, 2010, I was asked to give a speech for the Albuquerque TEA Party as part of the "Get Out the Vote Rally." I was honored by the request. The TEA Party group did not know me very well, had never heard me speak in public, and for all intents and purposes, I was a complete unknown to them. Those supposed damn racists wanted to put me on stage! What's up with that? The speech I delivered is in the Appendix.

Politics is Hard

As part of my transitional conversion process, I made the decision in late 2011 that I would get involved in local events in order to make a difference (at least in my local community). Obviously, my involvement in TEA Party activities connected me with an entirely different set of people. What I found was that the majority of these people shared similar views and values that I believed in. All of the TEA Party participants that Grasshopper and I met were average, middle-class, working folks, or recent retirees who had become frustrated by the continued progression of government intrusion into their daily lives.

While Liberals like to claim they are all about individual freedoms, they have no problem subjugating individual freedoms when the cause is deemed "for the good of the people." Take the example from the *NY Post* [Margolin, J.; Seifman, D., May 31, 2012] of "nanny" Mayor Michael Bloomberg, who wants to limit the sale and distribution of soft drinks greater than 16 ounces. Why? To stave off obesity in the city of New York. That's right, no more Big Gulps in the Big Apple. Why do liberal politicians believe it is within their purview to tell us what we can and cannot consume, smoke, drink, and eat? Why do they think they have the power to tell us what we can drive, how we can drive, and what we must wear when we drive? It seems to me that we have gotten away from requiring folks to take personal responsibility for their actions. Let's assume I decided I wanted to drink a 64-ounce cup of Coke while eating a large tub of butter-flavored oily popcorn to view the latest Blockbuster release from Hollywood. Let's also assume I drove to the theater on my Harley and I chose not to wear my helmet or leather chaps and I decide not to purchase insurance for the bike [in case you are wondering, I really don't own a Harley]. Who am I hurting? If I am willing to take the "known risks" associated with my behavior, then I should be held responsible for my actions. Drinking large cokes and eating fat-laden popcorn will eventually make you fat. Everyone knows this. Nevertheless, if that's the experience I want at a theater, then Nanny Bloomberg shouldn't have anything to say about it. Similarly, if I were to get in an accident while on the bike and I didn't have any insurance, then I should be prepared to get sued by an insurance company to pay for any damages and medical expenses out-of-pocket (assuming I survived the accident, since I wasn't wearing a helmet). We could have fewer laws if we put the onus and responsibility back on the individual and not on the "collective" society

I can hear the Liberals screaming already, "But what about the person who... [fill in your blank] can't afford to purchase insurance or is incapable of saying NO to large vats of popcorn." Simple, if you can't afford bike insurance, then don't own a bike. If you can't resist fatty popcorn, don't go to the movie! See, it's so simple for you to make the correct choice for yourself. Many issues can be handled simply though better communication and public service announcements to educate the public. Ultimately, behaviors can't be legislated, but education can shift public opinion and sentiment to move away from those things that are harmful to society. Education, and not legislation, is the key to changing behaviors. Liberals like Nanny Bloomberg don't understand the distinction.

It is because of people like Mayor Bloomberg showing up in local, city, and state government positions, that I felt I needed to get more involved in local politics. I needed to start paying attention to what was going on our local community and I needed to actively participate in the process. It just so happened that because I was involved in the local TEA Party events, an Albuquerque City Councilor, who asked to meet me for lunch, approached me in the fall of 2011. Personally, I was shocked, but also humbled by the fact that this person wanted to meet with me. Who am I to him? We met at a local Italian restaurant called Paisano's and I found him to be authentic, engaging, and extremely likable. He informed me that he was going to make a run for Congress in my District and that he wanted my support. That was welcome news to me because the current Democratic Congressman in my district was an Obama-Pelosi puppet. He was vacating his Congressional position to make a run for the vacant seat left by the Democratic senior statesman Senator Bingaman of New Mexico. I personally can't think of a single bit of legislation that my current Congressman supported that I agree with wholeheartedly. I was elated that the City Councilor was vying for the position from the Republican side. While the City Councilor never directly asked, I suspect he also wanted me to voluntarily work on his campaign. Frankly, I was surprised and honored by his request for my support. He is a good guy.

After speaking with the City Councilor, I walked away feeling validated that my voice was being heard. I told him that I needed to think about offering my support to him and that I would get back to him with an answer soon. I appreciated his honesty and integrity and I walked away thinking that here is a guy I could really support. Right about the same time, another friend of mine nicknamed MOTU (Master of the Universe) said that he was supporting another GOP candidate who was a former state legislator who was running for the same Congressional seat. MOTU said that he was on her volunteer campaign staff. He thought I would be a great addition to her team and asked if I would meet with her.

I'm thinking to myself, "Whoa, how often do you get to personally meet someone who is running for a Congressional seat and they want to meet you for lunch... NEVER!" So I told MOTU that I would meet with her and we arranged to have lunch at Paisano's again. This time around, I brought Grasshopper along. Maybe I shouldn't have, because at lunch, Grasshopper and the former state legislator hit it off right away. For a while, I couldn't get a word in edgewise and I became the odd man out. However, during the lunch, it became immediately clear to me that the state legislator had a lot of experience, having served four terms in the New Mexico state legislature. She was knowledgeable on issues, especially tax and energy policy (which was near and dear to my heart), and she clearly had the ability to understand the impact of conservative issues on the everyday lives of most people. This was only the second time I had seen this legislator. I remembered first seeing her during the primary race for Governor when she eventually lost out to the eventual winner Susana Martinez in 2010. Both Grasshopper and

I found this candidate to be engaging, articulate, well versed in New Mexico politics and having the same set of values that we shared.

All of a sudden, I had to make a choice. I liked both candidates. I decided that whomever I selected, I would volunteer my free time over the next eleven months to assist in their campaign. I actually was torn over whom to support. I prayed during the Christmas holiday to guide my decision, and ultimately after the New Year in 2012, I came to a decision to support the state legislator's campaign. I informed the City Councilor of my decision and let him know that if he won the primary election, I would willingly take up the banner and support him during the general election. The City Councilor was very gracious and stated that he looked forward to serving with me in the future. Politics is hard.

So, I joined the state representative's campaign and continue to support her as of the writing of this book. Turns out, I made the right decision, as she handily defeated her pre-primary opposition candidates by winning 62% of the delegates' votes. The City Councilor finished a distant second with 33% of the delegate vote. Soon after the pre-primary convention, the City Councilor withdrew from the race. I totally respect him for that decision. Ego and pride can sometimes get in the way of good decision-making. He had received enough votes to get on the primary ballot. It would have been a tough, uphill fight for him, and both camps would have needlessly spent limited campaign dollars beating up on one another. However, the real issue is winning the Congressional seat back from the

Democratic Party. With the City Councilor's departure, our candidate was unfettered and unopposed in the primary election. She is now poised to run against a slightly favored female Democratic candidate who went through a very tough primary fight. Our former state representative and her campaign support team will have their hands full for the general election. I have faith that she can rise to the occasion simply by explaining the differences in policy positions.

So what else have I been doing? The members of the campaign recognized early that G'hop and I weren't going to be full-time volunteers for their campaign. We both have full-time jobs that don't allow for a lot of volunteerism. Instead, G'hop and I decided to have a neighborhood "Meet and Greet" at our house one weekend, where neighbors could drop by to meet the candidate. This is a painless and relatively easy way for the local neighborhood to meet their candidate one-on-one and ask any questions they want in a safe environment. We had roughly 12-14 neighbors attend the event and by all accounts, it was pretty successful.

I decided to make a video for my candidate to show the campaign what I could do using rudimentary video editing tools. They liked it so much that it was immediately posted on their campaign website. Exciting. By default, I became part of their communication team. This is no easy chore. The campaign spinmeisters have to agree on the tone of and meaning behind the message. A well-run campaign has to be very strict with regards to messaging, because any mis-step can and will be used against you in a campaign. Case in point, in a recent press conference

179

[Tapper, J.; Bruce, M., June 8, 2012] President Obama announced that

> *"We've created 4.3 million jobs over the last... 27 months, over 800,000 just this year alone," the president said, "the private sector is doing fine. Where we're seeing weaknesses in our economy have to do with state and local government, oftentimes cuts initiated by, you know, governors or mayors who are not getting the kind of help that they have in the past from the federal government and who don't have the same kind of flexibility of the federal government in dealing with fewer revenues coming in."*

As you might imagine, the Romney campaign jumped all over this statement by the President that the "private sector is doing fine." My guess is this will be continually repeated between now and election night. Clearly, President Obama only considers public sector jobs as real. In Obama-world, unless you are kowtowing to the unions and creating more firefighters, policeman, or teachers positions, you aren't creating jobs? Never mind that public sector jobs come at the expense of private sector jobs... taxpayers, both individual and corporations, pay for these jobs. Clearly, the Progressives don't recognize that as important as these jobs are, the country will no longer be held hostage to union bosses seeking ever more entitlements for their constituency at the expense of the taxpayer. The Wisconsin Whipping by Governor Scott Walker and the people of that state sent a message loud and clear to union leaders everywhere. Enough is enough. Walker stuck to his principles and is turning that state around. He had to make tough choices and the results speak for themselves. Politics is hard.

As I continued to support our former state representative's campaign, I also decided I wanted to understand the whole delegate election process. To me this is a very arcane and convoluted process that is typified by the fact that most people in the general public (including myself) have zero understanding of the process. I wanted to know how one becomes a delegate in New Mexico, so in 2012, I set out on a journey to find out.

I went to a website that sort of explained the process and the calendar for 2012. The schedule was as follows:

April 2012 (tentative):

Republican Party Ward/Precinct Caucuses meet to choose the precinct's delegates to the County Convention. [Uniform State Rules of the Republican Party of New Mexico, Article 4-2-1(A)]

- There is no formal system applied in the Precinct Caucuses to relate the presidential preference of the Caucus participants to the choice of the precinct's delegates to the County Convention. The participants at each Precinct Caucus alone determine if presidential preference is to be a factor in such choice and, if so, how it is to be applied.

So I attended my Precinct caucus in April, (which wasn't very well advertised by the GOP) and those who attended had to vote for their delegates. It just so happened that in my precinct, we had more people show up than available slots. My local state representative was also present at this meeting. There was a ballot containing everyone's name that had registered. Votes were cast and counted and I happened to be one of the selected candidates from my precinct. Yippee! I am now a Republican precinct delegate. All I had to do was stand up and introduce myself. Who would have thought that it was that easy to enter into New Mexico politics? Now, on to the next step.

May 12 - 19, 2012:

County Conventions meet to elect delegates to the State Convention. [Article 3-2-1(A)].

- There is no formal system applied in the County Conventions to relate the presidential preference of the Convention participants to the choice of the Convention's delegates to the State Convention. The participants at each County Convention alone determine if presidential preference is to be a factor in such choice and, if so, how it is to be applied.

So, I register and show up at the local Bernalillo County convention. I expected this one to be tougher, given that there would be more people involved from the county. Interestingly, the publicity for this event was non-existent. If you weren't actively seeking to be a delegate, there was virtually no way for you to know about the whereabouts of this Convention. Here again, the event was not very well advertised. Now I understand why this process seems mysterious to everyone. What I discovered was, for my particular precinct, only five people showed up and we had something like 8 slots available and we were not allowed to act as surrogates for anyone else. Consequently, everyone who showed up at the County Convention in my precinct was automatically elected to the state convention. Wow! Just by showing up, I was now a County delegate and I get to attend the state convention to represent my county. How cool is that? Now, on to the next step.

June 5, 2012:

20 of 23 of New Mexico's delegates to the Republican National Convention are bound to presidential contenders based on the results of the voting in today's New Mexico Presidential Primary.

- 20 National Convention delegates are to be bound proportionally to presidential contenders who receive 15% or more of the primary vote statewide. [New Mexico Statutes §1-15A-9(c)(1)]

Today was the New Mexico primary election. Since my candidate was unopposed in her primary, most of us were focused on who would be her general election Democratic opponent and the results of the Wisconsin recall. Romney won the state, which means that initially, according to the stated rules above, 20 of 23 of NM's delegates are bound to presidential contenders.

June 9, 2012:

The New Mexico State Republican Convention convenes. The State Convention elects 20 delegates from New Mexico to the Republican National Convention according to the results of the primary. Voting is by secret ballot. [Rules Article 2-2-1(A)(2) and 2-2-10(D)(4)]

- The State Convention delegates gather by Congressional Districts to elect 9 National Convention District delegates, 3 from each of New Mexico's 3 Congressional Districts.

- The State Convention meets as a whole to elect the 11 National Convention At-Large Delegates. In addition, 3 party leaders, the National Committeeman, the National Committeewoman, and the chairman of New Mexico's Republican Party, will attend the National Convention as unbound delegates by virtue of their position.

- National Convention Delegates are bound for the first ballot unless released by the candidate. "The provisions of this section ... apply only to the first nominating ballot cast ... delegations may be released prior to the first ballot ... upon death of the candidate or upon his written unconditional release of such votes allotted to him..." [New Mexico Statutes §1-15A-9(d)]

A couple of weeks prior to the New Mexico state convention, I started receiving flyers, e-mails, and telephone calls from state delegates requesting that I vote for them to be a representative at the national convention either as an at-large delegate or as a Congressional District delegate as described above. So, here is the funny part. Since I was new to the process, I started thinking that since I won the county, it would be nice to be selected by the state to go to nationals in Tampa, Florida. I already knew I was a county delegate to go to the state convention. It never dawned on me that if I wanted to go on to nationals, I would have to do anything more than just show up and get people to vote for me. That is all I had to do the previous two times, why would I expect this time to be any different?

So what did I do? Well, I saw that interested delegates were actively contacting the other 500 delegates from around the state and asking for their vote. I decided to make a flyer describing who I am and I sent it out to the 500 delegates. "Vote for me to represent NM as a 2012 state delegate." I figured when I got to the state convention, I would hand out more flyers and try to get others to vote for me. I even had a logo designed for me to make it easier for people to recall my name.

On the day of the state convention, I show up and they have my name on the delegate list, but I have to register again. I was fairly sure I had registered in advance, but I didn't want to rock the boat, so I paid the $95 late registration fee. As soon as I finished registering, an attractive delegate seeking an at-large position approached me. She said she was a Delta Airlines flight attendant and that she recognized me from my flyer sent out earlier in the week. She asked me if I would support her, because she believed that regular folks should attend these events and not politicians. (I agreed with her sentiment and I did support her on my ballot). I also asked if she would reciprocate and support me. She said she would, and then she went to the names on the ballot and said that she couldn't find me on the ballot. I said "What?" She said "Your name isn't anywhere on the ballot. You need to report it." I started to laugh nervously and asked "Who would I talk to?" She said "You need to go to the Republican chair and see if they can resolve this immediately before the elections."

At this point, I started to wonder if I missed something. Maybe there is more to this than just showing up and asking for people's votes. I came across the head of the Albuquerque TEA Party, a friend of mine, who was on the ballot and I asked him if there was anything else I was supposed to have done to get on the ballot. He mentioned that there was a form that was supposed to be notarized and turned into the GOP office to ensure that you wanted to be on the ballot. I had no idea. He stated that the GOP office contacted him right before the deadline to ensure he wanted to be on the national ballot. Oh crap! I screwed up somewhere. Here I was, campaigning away like a wild man and I wasn't even on the ballot!! Rookie.

My dear friend, the Congressional candidate, showed up at the convention a bit later and someone told her that I wasn't on the delegate ballot. She apparently talked to a few of the party bosses and came back to me and said that she too had missed the deadline. So here we have someone who is running for a national Congressional seat, who also missed getting on the delegate ballot. Clearly, there is something wrong with a byzantine process where one of the Party's top candidates cannot understand or meet the requirements to become a national delegate.

In his defense, the Chair of the state GOP passed by to briefly chat with me at the convention and he said he would be willing to meet with me to discuss how to improve upon this process for future activities. Rather than get upset, I told him I would like to help him do that so that newcomers like me could better participate in the process. That is the engineer in me... I'm all about finding solutions to problems.

Funny, I had several people approaching me during the convention who stated that they would have voted for me. Although my chances to attend the National convention were slim, it would have been nice to try. Some delegates were concerned that I wasn't on the ballot. I explained that I obviously missed something in the process and that it was my fault. I suppose it is a good sign that I at least got my name out there for any future attempts at becoming a national delegate to represent my state. I even got to meet and shake the hand of the Lt. Governor of the state of NM who I believe has a promising future in politics.

To this day, I still don't know what I missed. Clearly, I bypassed something in the registration process or I just failed to register. Oops! Note to self: Next time you decide to venture out and campaign for a position, make sure your name gets on the stinking ballot!! Simpleton.

I have learned one thing from this... politics is hard.

Chapter 8

Grasshopper really respects Sarah Palin; so much so, that she dresses up as Sarah all the time. She walks around carrying her book and gives autographs when people stop her on the street. Not really, but she would, if I let her! I also have a tremendous amount of respect for Sarah Palin and the entire Palin family. The MSM was brutal to her and her family during the McCain-Palin campaign. However, Sarah continues to do her own thing and challenges the MSM by identifying and supporting conservative candidates to get elected. Is Sarah Palin a crazy woman like Grasshopper? You betcha, crazy like a fox.

What Do I Believe?

As my transformation from a liberal to a conservative continued, I had to ask a hard question of myself: "What do I really believe?" It's interesting, because if I had done this assessment when I was 27, my beliefs and attitudes at that time were still forming and my answers would be different. This exploration and understanding of how this country was created on the foundation of individual freedoms has changed my life and perspective forever. I guess the saying is true, "If you're not Liberal when you're 25, you have no heart. If you're not Conservative when you're 35, you have no brain." Clearly my brain didn't kick in until I was 52.

Early in my life, I sat back and asked myself, "What are my values?" After some serious soul-searching, I came to the conclusion that the things that I value in myself are the same things I value in others: honesty, integrity, and loyalty. That is also the order of priority I put on those values. So, in my day-to-day life, I strive to always be honest in my dealings with others. I also strive to have integrity in my dealings with others. If I say I am going to do something, I do my utmost to follow through. My word is my bond. And finally, I strive to be loyal in my relationships. Once I commit to a relationship with an individual (whether it is personal or professional), I will value and maintain the trust in that relationship. It is important to understand that I will only be loyal to the extent that it doesn't require me to be dishonest or lose my integrity, for I hold those values even higher.

I know these values are lofty. Have I always lived up to them? No way, Jose! Remember, I was a liberal for most of my life. However, I do have an inner compass that guides me when, or if, I stray from those values. I believe everyone has a value system that guides his or her daily decisions. It is really enlightening to ask the people you encounter on a regular basis what they value? You will learn lots about that person by asking that simple question. I certainly don't have any additional insight on how to live up to the values I seek to emulate. None of us is perfect. What I do know is that while I may falter from time to time, I will continue to get back up on that horse in order to live the perfect life.

What is my mission? To educate others and myself. Grasshopper likes to say that God is all knowledge. The more you know, the closer you are to God. There is not enough time on this earth to identify all the things about which I know nothing. The list is nearly infinite. While I have spent most of my career in the field of engineering, one of the things that I have come to appreciate is how little fundamental physics we actually know about engineering. Pick any topic on engineering and there are a multitude of unanswered questions. This is still a field ripe for additional understanding and innovation.

As my professional career begins to wane, my interests have begun to move from engineering to history and politics. Again, my lack of knowledge in this area would fill an ocean, but politics and the impact it has on our daily lives has fueled my passion for learning. As I study history, as I strive to understand the Constitution, as I read the Federalists papers, I begin to have a better appreciation of what our Founding Fathers intended. Part of my mission now is to continue my learning and, at the same time, try to bring others along, who can see that this country is on the wrong track. We already have the blueprint documents (the Deck-of-I and the Constitution) to put America on the right track. We just need to follow the blueprint.

What do I believe? I do believe in God, the Almighty. I believe that Jesus of Nazareth was the Son of God and that he died for our sins so that we could live in the Kingdom of Heaven. I am a Christian. I still have much work to do to become right with God. When I was younger, I use to believe that God was always on my side. As I continue to mature spiritually, I have come to the realization that I need to always be on His side. When I act and behave the way God wants me to, life becomes better for my family and me. Faith is a powerful force.

What do I believe? I am confident that my answers today are more seasoned. When I lamely attempted to put myself out there as a delegate for the state of New Mexico, other delegates asked me how I would vote on a particular issue. It quickly dawned on me that there are many people who are single-issue voters. If you don't agree with them on a particular issue, they won't vote for you regardless of your positions on other issues. I think that is why Liberals, Progressives, and Democrats continue to pit one group against another. Their strategy is guaranteed to find at least one issue upon which moderates or independents will disagree with a candidate, especially if that candidate is conservative (pro-life, pro-traditional marriage, pro-gun, pro-secure borders, etc.). That allows the single-issue voter to make a rational decision to vote for the liberal. The elegance of this strategy has worked for nearly 100 years for the Progressives. Predictably, we are just now beginning to see the road it is leading us down. A road filled with dependency, despair, depression, and despotism. If you don't think it can happen in America, visit Detroit and see America's future with 50 years of Progressive politics behind it. Conservatives need to emphasize that we support independence and liberty, not entitlements and servitude. Liberals promise their constituency a government check; conservatives promise their constituency a life free from government intervention, just as the Founding Fathers intended.

What are my thoughts on immigration? We have a significant illegal immigration problem in this country. At the same time, we have the most open legal immigration process in the world. According to the DHS Office of Immigration Statistics, naturalizations averaged about 680,000 people per year between 2000 and 2009. In 2011, the number of naturalized citizens was 694,193. The largest percentage of which is coming from Mexico.

According to the DHS [Lee, 2011]:

Naturalization is the process by which U.S. citizenship is conferred upon foreign citizens or nationals after fulfilling the requirements established by Congress in the Immigration and Nationality Act (INA). After naturalization, foreign-born citizens enjoy nearly all the same benefits, rights and responsibilities that the Constitution gives to native-born U.S. citizens, including the right to vote.

We do not have a *legal* immigration problem in this country. No other country even comes close to the United States for allowing immigrants to become citizens.

Clearly, there is an issue with the existing *illegal* immigrants, who were either brought here by their parents and who are, for all intents and purposes, contributing members of society. However, we cannot be the only country in the world that doesn't enforce its immigration laws. We need to develop a process to identify and create a path to citizenship for those already here. There are individuals, who, at a young age, were brought here through no fault of their own. At the same time, we need to find a balance that honors our legacy as a nation of immigrants, but also recognizes that we are a nation of laws. This is not an easy subject and reasonable people can agree on the goals, and still disagree on the process to get there. While I agree on the goal, any type of comprehensive reform on immigration must also include a clear drawing of the line on future illegal crossings. Maybe it's a one-time accelerated path to citizenship for those who have been here for more than 5 years and have no record of criminality, other than their illegal status.

I don't have the ultimate "silver bullet" solution. Many have tried and many have failed to reach a reasonable compromise on immigration reform. Marco Rubio, the senator from Florida, was leading a bi-partisan effort to create a piece of legislation to achieve such a goal. However, the Great One intervened on June 15th, 2012, and decreed a cabinet-level Dream Act.

What I do know is that what the President did on June 15th, 2012, is unconstitutional. He has no leeway to decide which laws he wants to enforce or not enforce.

Only monarchies have that authority. President Obama is not King Obama.

When it comes to principles, how do I decide on the best solution? I have decided that I am a Republican Conservative on social issues, I am a TEA Party Conservative on fiscal issues, and I am a Libertarian Conservative on business regulatory issues. Sometimes, these three philosophies are at odds with one another. When push comes to shove, I revert to the quote from Thomas Jefferson:

> *"The policy of the American government is to leave their citizens free, neither restraining nor aiding them in their pursuits."*

This is a hard pill for meddling politicians to swallow. Every problem does not require federal government intervention, nor does it require state intervention. Liberals want to solve every issue Americans face with legislation, regulation, taxes, and entitlements. That is not the role of government. The people, when left to their own devices, are quite apt at finding their own local solutions that work best for them.

The primary role of government is to protect individual freedoms. A secondary role is to provide for the common defense. The third and most abused role of government is to provide for the general welfare. Unfortunately, the Progressives have used the general welfare clause to insert all types of socialistic programs. Again, this was never the intent of the Founding Fathers.

What are my views on spending? This one is easy. You should not spend more money per year than your annual income can support. That includes taking on more debt (major purchases like an automobile or a home) should be limited, such that monthly payments can be made within your current income. No deficits. (Unfortunately, I have found that in speaking to the average person on the street, most people don't understand the difference between the government debt and the deficit.)

The best way to explain it is to imagine your uncle in the role of the government. Let's assume your Uncle Sam is the government. Uncle Sam has a spending problem. Let's put it in terms of numbers most households can appreciate. In 2011, you decide to examine your Uncle's budget and cash flow situation. Your Uncle Sam has an annual salary (income) of $23,035 per year. Unfortunately, Uncle Sam likes to buy things he can no longer afford and spends $36,031 per year. At the end of the 2011 year, Uncle Sam has a deficit of $12,996 for the year. Uncle Sam had to charge that deficit to his credit card and has been doing this for many years. He has built up a total debt (the cumulative total of his deficits from the preceding years), such that by the end of 2011, Uncle Sam owes the credit card company $148,000!! Geesh! This is nearly 6.5 times his annual income. At a minimum, and this isn't remotely possible, Uncle Sam would have to work for 6.5 years to pay back his creditors. Of course that would leave absolutely no money for anything else in Uncle Sam's life. Uncle Sam is now a slave to his creditors. In reality, Uncle Sam is not going to give his creditors all of his money for the next 6.5 years. Hence, the indebtedness will last much longer. Uncle Sam not only has to pay back this year's deficit, but he has to pay back his total debt with interest over the next several years.

After examining Uncle Sam's situation, you walk away shaking your head saying to yourself "My Uncle Sam is an idiot." Everyone knows that you cannot continue to spend more money than you bring in and not expect to pay dearly at some point. Either you default and declare bankruptcy (at which point no one will ever loan you money again), or you hunker down and dramatically cut your expenses and maybe get a second job to increase your income. Annual expenses should NOT exceed annual income. Further, it is prudent to put a little away in savings (a surplus) in the event of an emergency. Normal people do not continually add to their existing debt. Normal people, in order to pay DOWN their debt, either increase their income or reduce their expenses. Stupid Uncle Sam could increase his income (by expanding his business opportunities) and reduce his expenses (by eliminating unnecessary activities). He appears unwilling to do either.

If you multiply the above numbers by 100 million, you will have the situation America was facing at the end of 2011. Uncle Sam can no longer continue down this path. We are saddling the next generation of Americans with a credit card bill that previous generations and we created. This is why I believe in fiscal responsibility. Our generation has done a great disservice to future generations. It's time that we rectify the situation and put America on a path to no more deficits (balanced budgets) and use any and all surplus funds to retire our debt. We need to stop digging, and start filling the hole we have created for ourselves. The solution is simple math. Conservatives recognize this reality. Progressive politicians refuse to face this reality because it means no more cronyism, no more pay for play, no more union buyouts, and no more promises to their assorted constituencies.

The liberal, progressive, socialist ideologues presently in both Houses of Congress don't care about the facts. Their only interest is in maintaining and consolidating power. This is sad. It's time to get up and get active and to replace these destroyers of America with a new kind of citizen politician... it's time we identify people who put service ahead of politics. This is what I believe.

A Hint of Violence

Grasshopper Diary: January 11, 2011

I haven't written in a while. There are things I just need to get off my chest. Last Friday, some crazy lunatic shot a state representative in Arizona by the name of Gabby Gifford, a moderate Democrat, in the head. She was seriously injured and I pray for her recovery and health. Others were killed, including a federal judge and the representative's aide. It was despicable. What is even more despicable is the MSM's rush to judgment that the shooter was a TEA Party activist, that the shooter was a right-wing nut, that the shooter was encouraged by Sarah Palin, that the shooter was encouraged by Glenn Beck, that the shooter was encouraged by talk radio. Of course, none of this is true, but the left keeps at it.

Come to find out, the shooter was a left-wing psychopath. More importantly, he was just outright crazy. So, let's just blame the person who actually did it, the shooter. Wow, what a concept. I really wonder how some in the media sleep at night. I seriously do. I watch Glenn Beck every day and not once, not once, has he incited violence. In fact, during his 8/28 rally, he encouraged all of us to keep our cool, pray and give thanks. Why is that a threat?

I have not always been honest in my life, but I will tell you this, honesty is the best policy. I am married to the most honorable man I have ever met and he makes me a better person. He encourages honesty in me, he promotes my spirituality and my reverence of God. He keeps me grounded in life and comforts me when I am upset at the dishonesty that makes up most of our media. I pray for Sarah Palin and her family - considering the target the MSM has put on her. I pray for Glenn Beck and the courage he demonstrates daily to keep telling the truth - at a cost to both him and his family. I am frustrated, but I know I can look my opponents in the eye and tell the truth. The truth is powerful.

Grasshopper Diary: March 1, 2011

Ever since the Progressive Left and main stream media (MSM) felt obliged to blame right-wingers for the shooting of Rep. Gifford in Arizona and for stoking hate through uncivil discourse, there has been a spate of incidents, not generally acknowledged by the MSM of Leftists and Democrats urging violence. Here is a short list:

http://www.realclearpolitics.com/video/2011/02/23/union_member_assaults_freedomworks_employee.html

a union member assaults a FreedomWorks employee; and this,

http://www.realclearpolitics.com/video/2011/02/23/dem_congressman_to_unions_time_to_get_a_little_bloody.html

Rep. Michael Capuano (D-MA) tells union supporters, "Every once in a while you need to get out on the streets and get a little bloody when necessary." and this,

http://www.theblaze.com/stories/i-get-slammed-georgia-conservative-says-cop-refused-to-arrest-union-attacker/

a union supporter slams a TEA Party activist against a fence; and this,

http://www.theblaze.com/stories/fascists-go-home-tea-partier-injured-in-assault-by-teamster-at-sacramento-protest/

a TEA party member is injured by a Teamster; and this,

http://www.redstate.com/erick/2011/02/28/washington-posts-greg-sargent-demands-unions-get-violent-union-goons-attack-fox-reporter/

Washington Post's Greg Sargent demands unions get violent in Wisconsin.

I think what bothers me the most about all of this is that as a TEA Party member, I am vilified daily by the press at every opportunity with no proof. Here we have video after video after video of the violence and the hatred spewed by the unions and the Left. The excuse from the MSM is that this is just middle class America standing up for their rights. What rights? To bring this nation down? To suck the life out of every taxpayer? This country is in big, big trouble. The debt and deficit will be passed on to our children and our children's children. It is immoral. Socialism has been tried over and over again throughout history. It does not work.

I worry that today's youth have been indoctrinated with socialist views. That they have been taught that it is better to live by these words, "From each according to his ability, to each according to his needs" rather than understanding that with liberty comes responsibility. Individual freedom requires individual responsibility. The unions are mistaken when they claim that the politicians or the corporations want to take away their "rights." Rights do not come from the government or corporations. They come from God... life, liberty, and the pursuit of happiness. Unions and union members are no more entitled to higher wages and higher benefits than any other individual who can perform the same function at a lower rate. Free markets and capitalism are the best systems in the world. They allow for the creation of new wealth, eliminate industries and ideas that are no longer competitive, and advance the society by rewarding producers, which benefits everyone.

Example: Wal-Mart's success has resulted in the availability of more goods at lower prices for more people in our society. It has done all of this without unions. How is that bad?

Grasshopper Diary: May 16, 2011

I got patted down at the airport today for the first time since I have been flying back and forth between Fort Worth and Albuquerque. I always make sure I get in the line that doesn't require me to go through the millimeter wave scanner. It has nothing to do with modesty even though most folks refer to them as "naked" scan machines. I am not comfortable using them, because I fly twice a week and I've had a bout with cancerous melanoma. I'm not taking any chances with any kind of radiation. Anyway, this was the first time I got patted down and my behavior was ugly, ugly, ugly! I made snide remarks like "Are you enjoying this?" "Is this a dog and pony show?" I felt violated. Since it was my first experience receiving a pat down, I took it out on this poor TSA woman. She probably thought I was the biggest bitch in the world.

This was not her fault, but I sure blamed it on her. I asked God for forgiveness on the plane, but I need to ask it of her the next time I see her. I hope I don't have to go through that again. Nothing like a stranger feeling you up at 6:30 in the morning... Ugh! Does this sound like a police state to you or the land of liberty? I'm just asking?

This country is in grave danger, economically and politically. The solutions do not lie with the government, they lie with the people. I am a citizen not a subject. I can make my own decisions, good or bad. I don't need the government telling me what to eat, where to play, what car to drive, whom to be charitable to, etc. I fear this nation is on a path to tyranny.

The Founding Fathers knew that power in the hands of the people meant liberty. Power in the hands of the government is tyranny. When all hell breaks loose in this country, and it will, don't look to Washington, D.C. for assistance. I hope people are paying attention. All of the warning signs are in front of us.

This country is financially broke. Yet our President continues the outrageous spending on everything from NPR to Planned Parenthood to more government bailouts and everything in between. I'm a conservative, both socially and fiscally. And no, I don't want old people eating dog food in the street; I don't want women to forego cancer screening; and I don't want dirty air and water for every American. How stupid is that? Who wants those things?

We need leadership to reform and limit government expansion, or our children and our children's children will be indebted for their entire lifetime to a corrupt system. It is irresponsible for us to leave that legacy to the next generation. We need a true leader in the Executive branch. Barack Obama is NOT that leader. He is a joke. I hoped, like millions of other Americans, that he could have been the best President ever, but his ideology and divisive rhetoric of pitting one group against another is destroying this country. My warning for everyone is to prepare for major changes in this country regardless of who wins this election and future elections.

Ant's Parting Shot

As the 2012 Presidential campaign season approached the last 90 days, the Obama Administration appeared to be getting more desperate. Our Vice President, Joe Biden, made a racially inflammatory statement at a Danville, Virginia campaign stop in which he stated, verbatim:

> "They've said it. Every Republican's voted for it. Romney wants to let the – he said in the first 100 days, he's going to let the big banks once again write their own rules – unchain Wall Street. They're going to put y'all back in chains."

The audience he was speaking to was significantly composed of Black Americans. What did he mean by that? Was this another attempt to foster fear and hate amongst his constituents toward the Republican Party or just another "Uncle Joe" gaffe-tastic moment? Does Uncle Joe think that blacks fear that if they vote for a Republican, those very same Republicans will take the country back to slavery? Really? Reminders alert to Joe and the liberal media - it was Abraham Lincoln, a Republican, who signed the Emancipation Proclamation in 1863. The 13th Amendment of the Constitution to abolish slavery was passed by Congress with 100% Republican support and only 23% Democrat support in Congress. Not one Democrat either in the House or the Senate voted for the 14th Amendment of the Constitution declaring that former slaves were full citizens of the state in which they lived and were therefore entitled to all the rights and privileges of any other citizen of the state. By the way, not a single one of the 56 Democrats in Congress voted for the 15th Amendment that granted explicit voting rights to black Americans. Finally, it was Democrats in 1866 that formed the Ku Klux Klan as a means to intimidate blacks and white Republicans to pave the way for them to regain control in the elections. So, if anyone wants to put blacks back in chains, it's the Democrats.

I ran across an article entitled "Why I Do Not Like the Obamas" by Mychal Massie, a conservative commentator who just happens to be black. In this article, Mychal succinctly highlights the problem with the Obamas. He qualifies his dislike with

*"I don't like them, and I neither apologize nor retreat from my public condemnation of them and of his **policies**. We should condemn them for the disrespect they show our people, for his willful and unconstitutional actions pursuant to obeying the Constitutional parameters he is bound by, and his willful disregard for Congressional authority.*

*Dislike for them has nothing to do with the color of their skin, it has everything to do with their behavior, attitudes, and **policies**. And I have open scorn for their playing the race [card]." [Massie, 2012]*

Many Americans are waking up to the real Obama. His values are not American values. When he makes inane statements to hard working, successful Americans by exclaiming "If you've got a business – you didn't build that. Somebody else made that happen..." it should give one pause. He has little or no respect for what it takes to build and grow a business. He actually believes that those who do succeed, in some way, are not deserving of their success and are obligated to give back (in the form of additional taxes) to their government. It is unfortunate that we have a President who has zero understanding of the free market. It is unfortunate that we have a President who thinks that profits belong to the government and not to the businesses and employees that generated them. It is unfortunate that we have a President who would rather demonize, defame, and destroy the singular dream that makes America great - that anyone can be successful in America. It is unfortunate that we have this President.

Chapter 9

EPILOGUE

"Freedom is never more than one generation away from extinction. We didn't pass it to our children in the bloodstream. It must be fought for, protected, and handed on for them to do the same, or one day we will spend our sunset years telling our children and our children's children what it was once like in the United States where men were free."

–Ronald Reagan

I write this last section with trepidation. It is clear to me that the United States of America (US of A) is at a crossroad. Depending on the choices "we the people" make within the next few election cycles, determine whether the Progressive agenda will ultimately succeed at transforming this country to the Socialist Union of Amerika (SU of A).

To an informed observer, it is not obvious which path this nation will take. It is clear that the path chosen, once decided, will have a long-term impact on the lives and prosperity of future generations.

This country is polarized to the extremes. Progressives have a lock on the East and West coasts of Amerika. Liberal ideology, led by Progressive politicians promising cradle-to-grave entitlements for the underclass and disenfranchised are the norm on the two coasts. They subject their citizens to high unemployment, high taxes, and government dependency. These same politicians divide us into segments (rich versus poor, black versus white, women versus men, Christians versus Muslims, immigration versus border security, et al.) and it goes on and on and on. Why? Liberals, progressives, and socialists can only win elections when they divide and conquer. Their tactic is to pit one group against another. This diverts the attention of the masses away from a focus on their failed policies. To control a society, you must first divide it. The Progressive goal is to create a dependent class that relies on the government for everything. This dependent class becomes their voting bloc to remain in power. We now have a society in the US of A where nearly 50% of the people pay no taxes and yet receive some form of government assistance. We are at the crossroad of becoming the SU of A and the Progressives are well aware of the implications.

Liberal politicians love to vilify and tax the successful producers in our society. The entitlement mentality promoted by liberals is supported by the Hollywood elite on the West coast, who somehow feel liberal guilt for their success, and the so called Ivy-league intelligentsia on the East coast, who believe they are smarter than the masses and know what is best for the rest of us. A Pravda-like mainstream media machine supports all of this.

As shown in the chart [Trivisonno, 2012], we have over 46.4 million people on food stamps! One out of seven "Amerikans" are on food stamps. This is not the America I know. As I write this section, it appears that the Progressives are becoming more desperate. President Obama recently came out in favor of gay marriage. This has angered many blacks in America who are traditionalists when it comes to marriage. Why would he risk losing his traditional base on this issue? Because he knows many blacks will still vote for him based on color/race alone. Barack Obama is counting on the fact that to the average minority voter, he will appeal to them just because he himself is a minority.

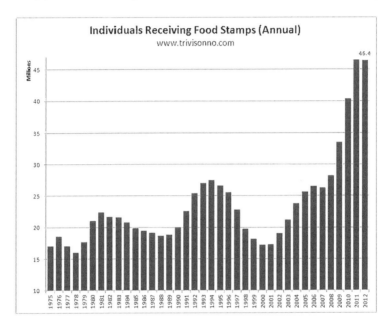

However, Barack Obama isn't like the rest of us. As of this writing, Obama has taken the unprecedented step by decree of a cabinet directive that allows scores of undocumented immigrants to stay here legally in the United States. Is he pandering for undocumented immigrant votes? President Obama announced that the U.S. will stop deporting DREAM Act-eligible youth. The current law requires his administration to deport illegal immigrants. Friday, June 15, 2012, may well be the point in Amerika's history where we went from America to Amerika. Whether you agree or disagree with the President's intent, it is clear that this President or any president, does not have the Constitutional authority to make laws. By this act, he has usurped the authority of the Congress and, in so doing, he has violated the separation of powers guaranteed by the Constitution. Is this an impeachable offense? When we are no longer a nation of laws, but a nation of men, we will become a nation of tyrants.

The Supreme Court decision on ObamaCare ruled that the mandate IS Constitutional because it is a tax. Hence, Congress can now require everyone to purchase something or be taxed. In my opinion, June 28, 2012 will go down in infamy as the date liberty died in America. While I cried, I gained some solace from Erick Erickson's article in *RedState* [Erickson, 2012] suggesting that Judge Robert is playing chess, while the rest of us are playing checkers. I must trust in God and pray Erick is right.

On June 28, Sarah Palin tweeted : *"Obama lied to the American people. Again. He said it wasn't a tax. Obama lies; freedom dies."*

I am not sure what to do about the Supreme Court decision on the ObamaCare Tax. While I understand Chief Justice Robert's logic in the decision, unlike Erick Erickson, I think the judge got it wrong. The Constitution was written to protect individual rights. The Constitution also gives Congress the power to tax. However, with this current ruling, Congress has the right to tax a non-event. If I choose NOT to do something, I can be taxed. Something doesn't smell right here. If I choose not to eat broccoli, because I don't like broccoli, the government can now tax me if they think I should be eating broccoli. Think about that for a second. There are a lot of things I choose NOT to do. If the government can tax me on any one of them, then the government owns me. I don't think that is, or was, the intent of the Founding Fathers. Chief Justice Robert's response is that the court is not responsible for judging the soundness of legislation, just to interpret it in the framework of the Constitution. He put the onus back on the people and the electorate. Basically, the Chief Justice of the Supreme Court is saying that if you don't want poor legislation, then it is up to you to elect quality officials. If you want more taxation, then continue to elect the same type of politicians who agreed to this law. Rather than defend the Constitution as he was appointed to do, the Chief Justice of SCOTUS told "we the people," it is in your hands now.

We had an opportunity to change course in the November 2012 election. Frankly, I'm worried that we have already passed the point of no return. In physics, there is a region around a black hole called the Schwarzschild radius. Everything that crosses that radius is forever lost to the known universe. The United States may have unwittingly crossed the Schwarzschild radius from a Republic to a Totalitarian state. We may have crossed the point of no return. Many of us realize that granting such all-encompassing taxing power to the government relegates all citizens as subjects of the state. We can turn this ship around, but we need a captain and a crew willing to make the effort to reverse course.

There is still hope. All is not yet lost for our country. The TEA Party-fueled "shellacking" in the 2010 mid-term elections showed that "we the people" will not stand idly by as our politicians drive us into a financial abyss. We are seeing signs of a revival. Governor Scott Walker's ability to beat back the election recall from the Unions in Wisconsin shows that the public is waking up. The ObamaCare tax is still unpopular. I pray that the recent Supreme Court ruling will fuel the flames of an outright mutiny of citizens from the Progressive agenda! I'm fed up that no one, not Congress, not the President, and now, not even the Supreme Court of the land, is willing to defend the Constitution that they swore to uphold. Chief Justice Roberts wrote, "It is not our job to protect the people from the consequences of their political choices." Okay. We get it. The Chief Justice has punted the ball back to the people.

James Madison, the father of the Constitution, wrote in Federalist No. 46, "The ultimate authority, wherever the derivative may be found, resides in the people alone." Our Founding Fathers knew that we the people must give our consent to be governed. No more. I refuse to give my consent to a tyrannical regime that no longer represents my values. I hope the rest of the country feels the same way.

Middle America (excluding Chicago) is finally pushing back. The people in the Deep South and southwest - where men are men and women are adored, where hard work is rewarded, and charity is a virtue - are determined to take this country back. Flyover country will no longer be ignored. The left-wing coasts may control the culture and the media, but flyover country establishes the traditions and values of this nation. Despite all attempts to transform this country to a godless, secular, morally depraved, and government-dependent society, the people in flyover country still respect God, hard work, the law, the Constitution, and their neighbors. The people in flyover country respect the flag, the men and women in the military, charitable giving, traditional marriage, and family. The people in flyover country represent the grit, talent, and individualism, which made this nation great.

"You and I have a rendezvous with destiny. We will preserve for our children this, the last best hope of man on Earth, or we will sentence them to take the last step into a thousand years of darkness."

- RONALD REAGAN 1967

The East and West coasts continue to cry out *"Hail our Pharaoh Obama! Hail our King Obama! Hail our Messiah Obama!"* Hailing Obama will lead to hell for America's citizens. It is time for the American people to wake up! I pray it is not too late for this great country, but we are at a crossroads. The decision is now. This nation still has a choice. Are we citizens or subjects? I am, and will forever be, a citizen. I proudly call myself a conservative. I will defend this country and her Constitution until my dying breath. May God Bless this country and keep her safe from harm.

Appendix

A SPEECH FOR FREEDOM

Hi, my name is Anthony. I would like to have a grown-up conversation with you. Like many of you, I have never been active politically, and like many of you, I trusted that the representatives in our local, state, and federal offices truly represented our interests and our values.

However, like many of you, I have had a growing sense of concern about the direction our country is headed. Something doesn't feel right.

The world around us is changing, and it bothers me that I am powerless to the gathering storm that is approaching.

I would like to tell you a story about my transformation. Six years ago, I met a woman who would eventually become my wife. I affectionately call her Grasshopper. Grasshopper and I began our journey in 2004. We used to meet regularly with friends to debate the issues of the day... politics, race, religion, and sex... all of the things one shouldn't discuss in mixed company, but we did. And what we discovered was that we had many differences in our worldview... our backgrounds were different, our cultures were different, and our perspectives on the world were different. And despite the fact that our differences were vast, our arguments served as a critical learning ground for both of us. As we passionately debated the issues of the day, there was a sense that we both believed in the greatness of America and what she stands for...

The more we learned, the more it became clearer to us that something was awry, and it wasn't about Democrats vs. Republicans. It took us over a year to realize that the establishment parties were nothing more than two sides of the same coin. The false debates only seemed to exist simply to get votes. As we discussed the issues, Grasshopper realized that the Republican ideas she believed in, people like George W., who supposedly represented the conservative right, continued to disappoint as he spent money like a drunken sailor while trampling on individual rights to privacy by signing the Patriot Act. Similarly, while I BELIEVED that the Democrats cared about the people, I came to the realization that what the Democrats really want is subjugation... they treat the populace as slaves by promising them cradle-to-grave social welfare dependency on the government all for the purpose of votes. The only way they can survive is to divide the people into false camps (the rich vs. the poor, the corporations against the unions, whites against minorities) and we see it daily on the news.

Ask yourself – "What is the difference between a "blue-dog" Democrat and a moderate Republican?"...absolutely nothing! It doesn't matter if they have a "D" or "R" next to their name. As you look at the results over the past 100 years, the net result is more government bureaucracy, more federal laws, more taxes, fees, and tariffs, and continued erosion of individual liberty. So today, Grasshopper and I have discovered a new truth - that we ARE in a war, and it is not a war between Democrats and Republicans. That is a false choice.

So what is this gathering storm? Imagine two mythological Greek gods in battle, the one on the Left has an army of Progressive Liberal Statists, who I call the PLS, and the one on the Right has an army of Constitutionally-Limited Conservatives, the CLC. That's YOU!! This is the battle we must fight, this is the battle we must win, and this is the storm we must survive to take America back.

So today, I have some good news and some bad news. Last month, Grasshopper and I attended the "Restoring Honor" rally in Washington, D.C. sponsored by Glenn Beck. On the plane, we met several folks from Albuquerque, who were also attending the rally. None of us had ever participated in anything like this before. That Friday, we watched the simulcast of America's Divine Destiny event at the Kennedy Center. It was a very moving and touching experience to see people from all faiths and denominations grace the stage and speak to our return to those ideas and values that made this country exceptional, and the singular point of agreement by all faiths is our reliance on God the Creator.

On Friday, one of the speakers at the Kennedy Hall, Richard Lee, spoke of autonomy. My wife looked at me strangely and asked what does that mean?

Autonomy, according to Webster, is the right of self-governance, freedom, and independence. This preacher stated that those on the Progressive left, want complete autonomy... freedom to do whatever they want as long as they don't hurt or infringe upon someone else's freedom. The Progressive Liberal Statist (the PLS) believe this is the ultimate utopia for mankind – freedom of choice, freedom from borders, freedom to define marriage between consenting adults, and freedom of speech – unless you disagree with them, then you are a bigoted, homophobic racist.

All of a sudden, like a lightning bolt, I had an epiphany - autonomy. Hell, we are on the same page. Constitutionally limited conservatives love autonomy. We believe in the rights of the individual, the right to bear arms to protect oneself, the right to do whatever we want, as long as it doesn't interfere with another's constitutional rights to life, liberty, and the pursuit of happiness. So, what is the difference? Since we both believe in Autonomy, and that Autonomy is GOOD, why all of the angst and consternation between the Left and the Right. Here is the rub... there is another word that starts with an "A" – authority. Who has the Authority, the power to enforce laws, to exact obedience, to command, determine, and judge?

The PLS, the progressive liberal statists understand that if everyone were truly autonomous, that the weaknesses and foibles of mankind are such that man's self-interest would ultimately lead to chaos and violence. Hence, the PLS believes that in order to limit self-interest and to encourage people to take care of those who can't, one needs an Authority to override the basic instincts of man. In their minds, that would be the government, who should have the right and the ability to coerce individuals to do things for the collective good of society. In their view, it is acceptable for the government to limit one's individual rights and to take the fruits of one's labor, because individuals cannot be trusted to do the right thing.

Our Founding Fathers understood this better than I could have possibly imagined. They understood that individual autonomy is GOOD. However, they also recognized that governments are also controlled by men, and that the inherent frailties and weaknesses of man will ultimately lead to corruption, a desire for more power, and a tyranny over the people that are governed. Our Founding Fathers were pious men, and they understood that man must appeal to a higher Authority, a moral Authority.

Call him God, Allah, Jehovah, the Lord of Nature, the ultimate Creator – it doesn't matter, as long as your God encompasses the supreme good in all mankind. And herein lies the difference. The Constitutionally-Limited Conservative, the CLC, believes the ultimate authority is in God, the Creator, as did the Founding Fathers. They believed that autonomy is good, as long as man regulates himself through a moral Authority. The CLC believes the collective good comes from our individual responsibility to a moral Authority to be charitable, to provide hope to those less fortunate, and to have faith in the goodness of mankind. We don't need government to tell us what to do - the government that governs best, governs least.

So here, right now, is our battleground. We believe in autonomy, we believe in fiscal responsibility, we believe in a constitutionally limited government, we believe in capitalism; but this is not enough. To win this war, we must show a reverence and deference to a supreme being, a God who appeals to the good in all of us, and that is what we learned at the Restoring Honor Rally.

We were energized by the number of people at the Rally (at least 500,000 people from all over the U.S. were in attendance). We met people from Connecticut, Michigan, Arizona, Pennsylvania, New Mexico, and Texas just within the small area we staked out. The sentiment was the same for everyone there… a sense that our country was not going in the right direction and that we need to restore America back to its roots.

Later that evening, we went to a well-known restaurant in Washington, D.C. It was crowded, so my wife and I sauntered up to the bar to get a drink while we waited for our reservations. Next to my wife, a grey haired, slightly round man, let's call him "Puffy Steve," had ordered an interesting flight of drinks in small wine glasses and my wife asked him what it was. Well, Puffy Steve, with this haughty tone in his voice, indicated that it was some sort of Pinot Noir with a highfalutin name, and then he said something amazing. He stated that he and his wife had just left another restaurant where there were a bunch of right-wing Glenn Beck nut-jobs. My wife looked at him, smiled, and calmly said "We were at the rally." Well Puffy Steve looked at her, then he looked at me and he said, "Oh you were at the Al Sharpton rally?" Now this is where things got interesting. I looked at him in the eyes and said, "No... we were at the Glenn Beck rally. We are one of those nut-jobs you just referred to!"

Puffy Steve then calls Jodi his wife over, a raven-haired plump woman (I'm not being derogatory... just descriptive), and he tells us that she will get a kick out of meeting us, as if we were some kind of circus show. As you might imagine, our conversation revealed a lot about the Washington, D.C. Establishment. We listened as they attempted to stereotype us. Of course, their first argument that we are all racists was... well, they couldn't say much of anything, because I'm staring right at them. Their second argument that we are homophobic was deflated when my wife revealed her adopted son was gay, and when those "arguments" didn't work, they accused us of trying to put religion into government and that they are firm believers of the separation of church and state.

It was clear we weren't making any progress with the discussion, so my wife shifted tactics. She asked plump Jodi "Do you know how many people were at the rally?" Jodi responded, "No." With pride in her voice, Grasshopper stated emphatically "Estimates are between 300,000 to 600,000 people were in attendance from all over the country." Jodi shrugged her shoulders "So what, who cares."

So, here is the bad news. The following day, we met for brunch at another couple's home that live in the D.C. area. They knew why we had traveled to D.C., and after spending more than two hours with them, not once did they ask about the rally - not once. That same evening, we met with another long-time friend who lives in the D.C. area, and again, not once did she ask us about the rally. Not once. Finally, my wife spoke up and said that the rally was AWESOME. Our friend said nothing. So, I chimed in and said, "I find it interesting that no one here in D.C. wants to talk about this rally where 500,000 people show up and no one mentions it." Our friend looked at us and said very matter-of-factly, "We have rallies here all the time. It's not a big deal."

So, there you have it, America. The people in D.C., within the Beltway, have grown tone deaf. It's not that they don't care, they are not even listening to "We the people" anymore. The elitist in Washington, D.C. live in an Ivory Tower, and the faint noises they hear from the outside are nothing more than a nuisance. We, the people, are insignificant. That night, in the hotel room, my wife cried. And as I went to sleep, I also cried.

The next morning, my wife awoke, her spirit renewed. She said, "I'm glad that I now know. The people here in D.C. don't care about us. I now understand what we have to do. We have to put people here who listen to us, and respond to us and who are above politics. People who will do the right thing for this nation - people who have honor. And we have to do it at the local, state, and federal levels."

Ladies and gentlemen, our journey will be long, our struggle will be hard, but the rewards of giving future generations a real shot at freedom and liberty is paramount. That's our message back to you.

A few weeks ago, I re-read the Declaration of Independence while on a plane. As I was finishing the declaration, I had a Glenn Beck moment, as tears ran down my eyes. For one brief moment, I put myself in their shoes. Picture this… these men, who were devoted to their country of origin, had a number of grievances that were being ignored by their government. They had tried on many occasions to get these grievances addressed, and yet their King rebuffed them at every attempt. These men knew, by signing this Declaration of Independence against the most powerful military nation on earth, that for the remainder of their lives, they would be deemed enemies and criminals of the state. They were in effect, signing their own death warrant. And the only thing they could depend on was each other and their faith in God - all for the cause of liberty.

"… And for the support of this Declaration, with a firm reliance on the protection of divine Providence, we mutually pledge to each other our Lives, our Fortunes and our sacred Honor."

Today, I ask the question, "Are WE prepared to do the same?"

I would like to end with a quote from Abraham Lincoln… the words he spoke on November 19th, 1863, at Gettysburg still hold true today, for our America.

"…our fathers brought forth on this continent, a new nation, conceived in Liberty, and dedicated to the proposition that all men are created equal.

Now we are engaged in a great civil war, testing whether that nation or any nation so conceived and so dedicated, can long endure. We are met on a great battlefield of that war…. a final resting place for those who here gave their lives that that nation might live. It is altogether fitting and proper that we should do this.

But, in a larger sense, we cannot dedicate – we cannot consecrate – we cannot hallow – this ground. The brave men, living and dead, who struggled here, have consecrated it, far above OUR poor power to add or detract.

The world will little note, nor long remember what we say here, but it can never forget what they did here. It is for us the living, rather, to be dedicated here to the unfinished work which they who fought here have thus far so nobly advanced. It is rather for us to be here dedicated to the great task remaining before us – that from these honored dead we take increased devotion to that cause for which they gave the last full measure of devotion – that we here highly resolve that these dead shall not have died in vain – that this nation, under God, shall have a new birth of freedom – and that government of the people, by the people, for the people, shall not perish from the earth."

Ladies and gentlemen… THAT IS OUR CHALLENGE!

Cited Works

Bai, M. (July 25, 2010) "POLITICAL TIMES; When It's About Race, It's Probably About Age, Too."

Banfield, E. C. (1970). The Unheavenly City; the nature and future of our urban crisis. Boston, Little.

Central Texas 9-12 Project, (September 5, 2010), http://www. breitbart.com/Big-Government/2010/09/05/Restoring-Honor-Rally-Changes-Hearts-and-Minds

Erickson, E. (June 28, 2012) "I'm Not Down on John Roberts." http://www.redstate.com/erick/2012/06/28/im-not-down-on-john-roberts/

Folkenflik, D. (October 21, 2010) "NPR Ends Williams' Contract After Muslim Remarks." http://www.npr.org/templates/story/story. php?storyId=130712737

Fox News (July 5, 2010) "NASA Chief: Next Frontier Better Relations With Muslim World." http://www.foxnews.com/ politics/2010/07/05/nasa-chief-frontier-better-relations-muslims/%23ixzz1xExUsoai

Gabbay, T. (April 9, 2012) "'Race Wars' Part 1: The Shocking Data on Black-on-Black Crime."

Griffin, G. E. (2002). The Creature From Jekyll Island "A Second Look at the Federal Reserve", American Media.

Henry, P. (May 12, 2012) "White Reporters' Beating by Norfolk Black Gang Ignored by Media, but Real Question is, What is Happening to America's Cities?"

Hernandez, G. (2009) "Academy Awards 2009: Sean Penn wins the Oscar for "Milk" and says: "We've GOT to have equal rights for everyone…"."

Lee, J. (April 2011) Annual Flow Report U.S. Naturalizations: 2010, Office of Immigration Statistics, Department of Homeland Security

Levin, M. (2009) Liberty and Tyranny "A Conservative Manifesto", Threshold Editions.

Janis Diary, (August 17, 2010) "It's Time This Was Said–And I'm Saying It." Redstate.com http://www.redstate.com/janis/

Malkin, M. (February 10, 2012) "'To Stop the Multiplication of the Unfit'."

Margolin, J.; Seifman, D. (May 31, 2012) "Mayor Bloomberg wants to impose 16-ounce limit on sugar drinks." http://www.nypost.com/p/ news/local/supersize_smack_TebHeJsmQxoOjqawvfuXRL

Martin, J. (2010) "Bill Maher: The Tea-baggers named themselves after a gay sex act, they aren't too bright."

Massie, M. (February 22, 2012), http://mychal-massie.com/premium/why-i-do-not-like-the-obamas/

Nell, W. C. (1855). The Colored Patriots of the American Revolution. Boston, Robert F. Wallcut.

Paul, R. (2009). End the Fed, Grand Central Publishing.

Project, T. C. T.-. (September 5, 2010) "Restoring Honor Rally Changes Hearts and Minds."

Rand, A. (1957). Atlas shrugged. New York, Random House.

Rasmussen, S. (2012). Rasmussen: Most Americans Below Poverty Level Have Enough Food, at Least One Car. Newsmax. http://www.newsmax.com/US/Rasmussen-poverty-level-book/2012/02/01/id/426339, www.newsmax.com.

Rubyman, M. (2002) "Janeane Garofalo: Flag-Burning Chokes Me With Pride."

Skousen, W. C. (2009). The Five Thousand Year Leap "28 Great Ideas That Changed the World", American Documents Publishing, L.L.C.

Smith, J. (2009) "Pharaoh's Economic Stimulus Package," http://www.sermoncentral.com/sermons/scripture/sermons-on-genesis-47.asp

Tapper, J. March 15, 2012, "Four Questions for Bill Maher," http://abcnews.go.com/blogs/politics/2012/03/four-questions-for-bill-maher/

Tapper, J. ; Bruce, M. (June 8, 2012) "President Obama Says The Private Sector Is Doing Fine." http://abcnews.go.com/blogs/politics/2012/06/president-obama-says-the-private-sector-is-doing-fine/

TeabagFoxNews.com (2009). Janeane Garofalo calls tea baggers "racist rednecks". http://www.youtube.com/watch?v=Ms45EzMR0f8, YouTube.

Thornton, A. (2011). AntTV. http://www.youtube.com/user/icesaint2011/videos.

Trivisonno, M. (2012) "Individuals Receiving Food Stamps (Annual)." http://www.trivisonno.com/food-stamps-charts

Wiedemer, D. W., Robert; and Spitzer, Cindy (2011). Aftershock: Protect Yourself and Profit in the Next Global Financial Meltdown. John Wiley & Sons, Inc.

Woods, T. E. (2009). Meltdown: A Free-Market Look at Why the Stock Market Collapsed, the Economy Tanked, and Government Bailouts Will Make Things Worse, Regnery Publishing.

Made in the USA
San Bernardino, CA
18 January 2017